AGRICULTURAL WORKERS
IN THE U.S.S.R.

THE CONTEMPORARY SOVIET UNION SERIES:
INSTITUTIONS AND POLICIES

Each volume in the Contemporary Soviet Union Series examines in detail the facts about an important aspect of Soviet rule as it has affected the Soviet citizen in the 50 years since the Bolshevik Revolution of 1917.

Subjects include industry, culture, religion, agriculture, and so on. A careful examination of official Soviet material in each field provides essential basic reading for all students of Soviet affairs.

Robert Conquest is a former Research Fellow in Soviet affairs at the London School of Economics and Political Science and Senior Fellow of Columbia University's Russian Institute. His works include *Power and Policy in the U.S.S.R.*, *The Pasternak Affair: Courage of Genius*, *Common Sense About Russia*, *The Soviet Deportation of Nationalities*, and *Russia after Khrushchev*.

THE CONTEMPORARY SOVIET UNION SERIES:
INSTITUTIONS AND POLICIES
EDITED BY ROBERT CONQUEST

Agricultural Workers
in the U.S.S.R.

FREDERICK A. PRAEGER, *Publishers*
New York · Washington

BOOKS THAT MATTER

Published in the United States of America in 1969
by Frederick A. Praeger, Inc., Publishers
111 Fourth Avenue, New York, N.Y. 10003

Introduction © 1968 in London, England, by Robert
Conquest

Library of Congress Catalog Card Number: 68-31528

Printed in Great Britain

Contents

Editor's Preface

This book concerns itself with the condition of the agricultural workers in the Soviet Union, rather than with the broader theme of the development of Soviet agriculture as a whole.

But the unsatisfactory nature of the system in human terms is inextricably involved with its productive inefficiency. As Academician Sakharov remarks in his celebrated essay 'Thoughts on Progress, Peaceful Co-existence and Intellectual Freedom' now circulating in Moscow, it has not been merely a question of 'unconstrained exploitation of the countryside, predatory procurement at "symbolic prices"... the near-serfdom of the peasantry, the appointment of *kolkhoz* chairmen solely on the basis of their servility and cunning', but also 'a most profound and scarcely retrievable destruction of the economy and the whole way of life of the countryside'.

The collectivisation carried out in 1930–3 was above all a war to bring the peasantry, and agricultural production, under party and state control. And the casualties were those of a major war.

The political target was reached. The same does not apply to the economic. The economic destruction was on a par with the human casualties. Over a quarter of the productive capacity of the farms was destroyed—in particular, the decline in livestock was catastrophic: cattle dropped from 67 million in 1929 to 38 million in 1933,* and horses from 32 million to 17 million.† Worse still, in the long run, the new system proved incapable, even after many years, of producing the grain and meat surpluses planned and required.

Forced collectivisation was not a necessary consequence of Communist—of Leninist—ideas. Lenin warned against any but a long process of persuasion and education in bringing socialism to the countryside, and the party line till 1929 followed his

* (Summer figures) *The USSR in Figures*, Moscow, 1935, pp. 110, 180 ff.
† Chislennost Skota v SSSR. Moscow, 1957, p. 6.

advice, against the more extreme ideas of the 'left' faction around Trotsky.

But even they, the original theorists of the idea of wringing the resources for industry from the countryside like Preobrazhensky, had, as a matter of simple calculation, intended to combine this 'socialist exploitation' with fiscal measures designed to encourage agriculture. Stalin's collectivisation, considered from this point of view as a means of financing industrial progress by funds from the agricultural sector, was simply a failure—a reckless, ill-conceived, crudely executed failure.

The Japanese had been faced with the same problem from the beginning of the Meiji epoch. The Government had to look to the village as the source of the savings needed to finance the new industry. As a result, up to 60 per cent of the peasants' income was taken from them in tax and rent.* But at the same time the Japanese authorities gave them every incentive to improve techniques and increase production. Between 1885 and 1915 the productivity of agricultural labour about doubled, farm output increased by 44 per cent and per capita food production by 20 per cent.† Without compulsion, or forced labour, simply by fiscal means, accompanied by government activity in credit, roads, water supplies, and technical help, the agricultural sector was kept economically healthy, and able to play its part in the national modernisation.

The Japanese line was naturally not without faults and distortions, and need not be offered as an absolutely valid model for other countries in such a position. But at least, and long before Stalin's extravagant initiative, it shows the main consideration, economically speaking. And basically, this is an old and simple point: that excessive taxation destroys the sources of revenue.

At the Central Committee plenums of September, 1953, and February, 1954, Khrushchev revealed that grain production was still less per capita, and cattle figures less absolutely, than in Tsarist times. On January 1, 1916, there were 58,400,000 cattle on the present territory of the USSR; on January 1, 1953, 56,600,000: the population had meanwhile gone up from under

* W. W. Lockwood, *The Economic Development of Japan, Growth and Structural Change, 1868–1938*, OUP, 1955, pp. 26, 56.

† B. J. Johnston, *Journal of Political Economy*, 1951. *See* S. Swianiewicz, *Forced Labour and Economic Development*, OUP, 1965, for a discussion.

160 million to almost 190 million. Again, in spite of a vast effort of capital and technical investment, the yield in 1965 of 950 kilograms per hectare was small improvement on the 1913 figure of 820 kilograms.*

Soviet literature of the late Thaw often pointed out that the old-time peasant had more genuine sense of agricultural needs than is found at the present. A recent Soviet story even makes the point that a collective farm disaster—the death of a herd of cows through gorging on damp clover—could not have happened even under the landlords of Tsarist times. It took place when the kolkhoz chairman was off duty, at the weekend. "Can anyone imagine a landowner keeping a bailiff who resided permanently in town and went off home like an office worker even when summer work was in full swing . . .?'†

There is no reason, if a free choice of method were allowed, why the Russian land should not be as productive and prosperous as the equivalent territories of Canada and the USA. Even today, about a third of all Soviet agricultural output still comes from the peasant's exiguous private plot and private cattle. A recent Soviet novel about a collective farm in the north even shows a 67-year-old *kolkhoznik*, retired through rheumatism, making a better living from his private patch of vegetables than the rest of the *kolkhoz* members can achieve.‡

It seems to have been precisely because of its irrationality and bloodiness that collectivisation became a dogma impossible to dispute. Pasternak doubtless exaggerated when (in *Doctor Zhivago*) he attributed the whole Terror to the fact that 'collectivisation was both a mistake and a failure, and because that couldn't be admitted, every means of intimidation had to be used to make people forget how to think and judge for themselves . . .'. But it is clear that to write it all off cheerfully as an unfortunate mistake is something beyond even the capacity of the *apparat*. For it would be a confession of at best criminal negligence or manslaughter.

The millions who perished, the millions who suffered under this new and dreary serfdom—to admit that this was all in vain, to revert (as in Yugoslavia and Poland) to a method at once more productive and less oppressive, seems to require an effort beyond the moral strength of the Party responsible—many of

* *Narodnoye Khozaistvo SSSR v 1965 godu*, p. 311.
† Yefim Dorosh, "Rain and Sunshine", *Novy Mir*, no. 6, 1964.
‡ Fyodor Abramov, "Round and About", *Neva*, January, 1963.

whose current leaders played active, if minor parts in the original campaign. The burden cannot, it seems, be faced.

From 1954 to 1958 a sensible improvement took place. It came in the main as the result of abandoning the elements of Stalin's rural system which were wholly unjustifiable even on its own principles. Once these absurdities—such as the taxes which, as Khrushchev tells us, were actually larger than the peasants' entire cash income—were removed, and the villages had been advanced from near-starvation to mere poverty, the end of the possibilities of advance within the system was soon reached. From 1958 agricultural output has been virtually stagnant. The solution—many and various "reorganisations"—has not proved efficacious.

During the Stalin period grain statistics were falsified by the "biological yield" method. Estimates of the crop in the field were substituted for the actual count of grain in the barns. As Khrushchev later revealed, this led to an exaggeration in 1952, for example, of a harvest of about 92 million tons being presented publicly as 130 million.

The method was abolished after Stalin's death. But the system at present in use is, if not so scandalous, still a remarkably unsatisfactory one. Under it the crop is measured cut on the ground, or in the bins of the combine harvesters, before transport, drying and the removal of dirt. It seems that a loss of up to 20 per cent by weight is implied. But this is only one of the dubious methods by which an admittedly unsatisfactory situation is made to appear nearly tolerable.

For many decades, Soviet official statements on agriculture have concentrated on much-publicised plans for huge advances, punctuated by rather quieter admissions that the last one has proved largely abortive. Khrushchev's announcement of May, 1957, that the USSR would catch up with America in meat and milk production within the next two or three years* was only one of a series of chimeras. For the present the more extreme of these have been abandoned, and a certain reversion to the remaining possibilities of rationalisation within the system is producing marginal gains, though nothing resembling the radical improvement required and promised.

Instead, as we shall see, the rural economy is subjected to bureaucratic reorganisations, at best tending towards minor and

* *Pravda*, May 24, 1957.

comparative devolution. As long as the present *kolkhoz* system persists, it is difficult to imagine more than minor improvement. Meanwhile the peasant remains a second-class citizen both in status and economically, and agriculture by far the most backward in the civilised world. All in all, except for the Secret Police itself, no single one of the institutions of the Soviet Union has brought the régime less credit than the collective farm.

Acknowledgements are due in the first place to H. S. Murray; and also to Dr. A. Alexeyenko and M. Friedman.

ROBERT CONQUEST

I

Historical Development
to the Death of Stalin

The Marxist view of the peasant was traditionally an unflattering and unsympathetic one. Deemed no true revolutionary, he was relegated to a secondary rôle—at best that of an unreliable ally of the industrial proletariat. He could only improve his lot by becoming proletarianised. This attitude is seen in the Communist Manifesto of 1848,[1] which declared: 'The proletariat alone is a really revolutionary class. The other classes decay and finally disappear.' The peasantry were lumped together with other sections of 'the lower middle class', which 'are not revolutionary, but conservative. Nay, more, they are reactionary ... If by chance they are revolutionary they are so only in view of their impending transfer into the proletariat.'

The manifesto listed among the measures to be taken after the seizure of power by the proletariat:

'Abolition of property in land ... the improvement of the soil generally in accordance with a common plan. ... Establishment of industrial armies especially for agriculture. Combination of agriculture with manufacturing industries; gradual abolition of the distinction between town and country.'

Characteristic of Marxist teaching on agrarian problems was its insistence on the superiority of large-scale over small-scale farming, and on the need to replace smallholdings, after the proletarian revolution, by large-scale co-operatives. According to Engels, who elaborated this point in *The Peasant Question in France and Germany* (1894),[2] the transformation should be achieved without the use of force:

'When we are in possession of State power we shall not even think of forcibly expropriating the small peasants (regardless of whether with or without compensation), as we shall have to do in the case of the big landowners. Our task relative to the small peasant consists, in the first place, in effecting a transition of his private enterprise and private possession to co-operative ones, not forcibly but by dint of example and the proffer of social assistance for this purpose . . . We, of course, are decidedly on the side of the small peasant; we shall do everything at all permissible to make his lot more bearable, to facilitate his transition to the co-operative should he decide to do so, and even to make it possible for him to remain on his smallholding for a protracted length of time to think the matter over, should he be still unable to bring himself to this decision.'

Engels considered[3] optimistically that even the well-to-do peasants would probably transfer voluntarily to co-operatives, so that force would only have to be applied against the big landlords.

LENIN AND THE PEASANT

Marxist revolutionary doctrine, which focused on the urban proletariat and largely ignored the peasantry, was hard to apply in Russia, where land-hungry peasants dominated the scene and the peasant had habitually been regarded as the main instrument of revolution. Lenin's earliest political writings were devoted to combating such 'populist' views. He was deeply imbued with the Marxist disdain for the peasantry, because of its attachment to private property, individualism, and conservatism. But he realised, especially after the peasant upheavals of 1905, the need for peasant support for the proletarian revolution, and evolved the idea of a 'worker-peasant alliance' in which the worker remained very much the senior partner. He continued to demand the abolition of all private property in land and it was not until shortly before the Bolshevik Revolution, as a tactical expedient, that he gave all-out support to the slogan: 'Land to the Peasant'. By sanctioning and encouraging the peasant seizure and division of land to secure Bolshevik power in 1917, Lenin postponed and made more difficult the goal of large-scale co-operative agriculture.

The Bolsheviks were so weak in rural areas that at first they had to collaborate with the non-Marxist, peasant-supported Socialist Revolutionary Party, whose agrarian programme they temporarily took over. The first agrarian measures adopted under the Soviet régime were Socialist Revolutionary, not Bolshevik in inspiration, and were framed in response to peasant demands rather than in conformity with Bolshevik doctrine about the 'socialisation of agriculture'.

Thus the Land Decree of November 8, 1917, incorporated the Socialist Revolutionary 'Peasant Instructions', which had been drawn up on the basis of peasant demands.[4] It declared that only the Constituent Assembly (to be dispersed by the Bolsheviks when it met in January, 1918) could decide the land question, but asserted that 'the most just solution' would be the conversion of all land, including State land, 'to the use of all who work on it', and that 'forms of land tenure must be completely free... as may be decided by individual villages'. A decree 'on the socialisation of land' of February 19, 1918,[5] while referring to the virtues of a collective system of agriculture, was concerned to achieve the just distribution of land according to the Land Decree. Lenin subsequently admitted:

'We Bolsheviks were opposed to the law. Yet we signed it, because we did not want to oppose the will of the majority of peasants ... We did not want to impose on the peasants the idea that the equal division of the land was useless, an idea which was alien to them. Far better, we thought, if, by their own experience and suffering, the peasants themselves came to realise that equal division is nonsense ... That is why we helped to divide the land, although we realised it was no solution.'[6]

Lenin was concerned, where possible, to avoid antagonising the peasantry since his régime depended on it for survival—as food-provider and for Red Army recruits. He consistently counselled against haste and coercion in the 'socialisation of agriculture', and the first experiments in this direction—the setting up of collective and State farms,* communes and other forms of collective agriculture—made little headway. It was not 'socialisation' but Bolshevik measures for securing food during the civil war—in particular, their use of armed detachments to extract grain by force and the 'food dictatorship'—that alienated the peasantry. Lenin tried to maintain some allies among the peasantry by 'splitting' it, and drawing a largely artificial distinction between poor and middle peasants with whom the Bolsheviks allegedly collaborated, and *kulaks* who were blamed for the famine and held to be legitimate

* Known in Russian respectively as *kolkhoz* (abbreviation of *kollektivnoe khozyaistvo*) and *Sovkhoz* (abbreviation of *Sovetskoe khozyaistvo*).

targets for repression. But the combination of a desperate food situation and serious peasant uprisings in 1920–21 (the most important of which, led by Antonov, had two 'armies' in the Tambov area totalling at least 50,000 men, and had to be suppressed by the Red Army under Marshal Tukhachevsky) made further radical concessions to the peasantry necessary.[7] This was the New Economic Policy (NEP) which replaced the compulsory grain deliveries by a tax in kind and granted increasingly important concessions to private enterprise, including even the right of peasants to hire labour and lease land.[8]

Under NEP, agricultural production recovered and the peasants were pacified. Lenin claimed in November, 1922:

'Peasant uprisings which, before 1921, were a common occurrence in Russia, have almost completely ceased . . . The position of the peasant is now such that we have no reason to fear any movement against us from him . . . Any serious dissatisfaction with us on the part of the peasantry as a whole is at any rate completely out of the question. This has been achieved in the course of one year.'[9]

AGRARIAN POLICY AND THE
POST-LENIN POWER STRUGGLE

The policy of conciliating the peasants was continued after Lenin's death in January, 1924. In the spring of 1925, it was taken even further when Bukharin, supported by Stalin, launched a campaign to encourage efficient and well-to-do peasants (i.e. *kulaks*) to expand and develop and thereby bring about a national economic revival. The most memorable episode in this campaign was a speech by Bukharin in the Bolshoi Theatre in Moscow, when he said:

'Our policy in relation to the countryside should develop in the direction *of removing, and in part abolishing, many restrictions which put the brake on the growth of the well-to-do and kulak farm*. To the peasants, to all the peasants, we must say: *Enrich yourselves*, develop your farms, and do not fear that restrictions will be put on you. However paradoxical it may appear, *we must develop the well-to-do farm in order to help the poor peasant and the middle peasant*.' (Emphasis as in *Pravda*.[10])

Bukharin denounced as 'theoretically incorrect and practically senseless' the view that 'capitalism is developing in the countryside, that the *kulak* will establish large-scale farming, that renting will grow, that the *kulaks* will turn into new landlords and that we shall then have to carry out a second revolution on the rural front'.

This, however, was the high-point of the conciliation policy. The controversy over agrarian problems was one of the central issues in the post-Lenin power struggle. Its main feature was Stalin's attack first on 'Leftist' and then on 'Rightist' opponents and, in line with this manœuvre, his gradual abandonment of the view that the expansion of industry required the development of a prosperous peasant economy through concessions to the peasants. He came to espouse the opposite view: that industrialisation must take place at the expense of the peasants. Already, before the end of 1925, Bukharin had been compelled to retract[11] his slogan 'Enrich yourselves'.

The swing away from conciliation was hastened by the fact that although agricultural production increased under NEP, so did difficulties in getting the peasants to market it. In 1928, according to Stalin, 'the amount of marketable grain in our country is now half what it was before the war, although the gross output of grain has reached the pre-war level".[12] Stalin blamed the procurement crisis mainly on the *kulak* and said that 'the solution lies in the transition from individual peasant farming to collective, socially-conducted agriculture', and in 'a struggle against the capitalist elements of the peasantry, against the *kulaks*'.[13] The main victims of this policy switch were precisely those peasants whom the régime had previously encouraged to expand.

Stalin's justification of his policy before the Central Committee at a July, 1928, plenum was published more than 20 years later. It exemplifies his superficial and schematic style of argument, but is the frankest apologia which he left on record:

'The way matters stand with the peasantry in this respect [capital accumulation for investment in industry] is as follows: it not only pays the State the usual taxes, direct and indirect; it also *overpays*—in relatively high prices for manufactured goods, in the first place, and it is more or less *underpaid* in the prices for agricultural produce, in the second place.

'This is an additional tax on the peasantry for the sake of developing industry, which serves the whole country, including the peasantry. It is something in the nature of a "tribute", of a supertax, which we are temporarily compelled to levy in order to maintain and develop our present rate of industrial development, in order to ensure an industry for the whole country, further raise the well-being of the rural population and then abolish altogether this additional tax, these "scissors" between town and country:

'It is an unpleasant business, there is no denying. But we should not be Bolsheviks if we slurred over this and closed our eyes to the fact that, unfortunately, our industry and our country cannot *at present* dispense with this additional tax on the peasantry . . .'

With less candour, Stalin continued:

'Are the peasants capable of bearing this burden? They undoubtedly are: firstly because this burden will grow lighter from year to year, and secondly, because this additional tax is being levied . . . under Soviet conditions, when exploitation of the peasants by the Socialist State is out of the question, and when this additional tax is being paid in a situation in which the living standards of the peasantry are steadily rising.'[14] (Stalin's emphasis.)

Bukharin, according to Stalin, made the 'ludicrous accusation' that this policy amounted to 'the military and feudal exploitation of the peasantry' and denied that the establishment of collective and State farms could 'play any serious part in the development of our agriculture'.[15] With even greater prescience, Bukharin told Kamenev that Stalin would 'have to drown the risings in blood'.[16] But all objections were futile; by November, 1929, Bukharin had been removed from the Politburo and compelled to publish a grovelling recantation.[17]

In 1928, 'emergency measures' for the forcible extraction of grain, similar to those employed during the civil war, were taken to deal with the crisis, which Stalin admitted was not merely economic but contained a political threat to the régime.[18] These repressive measures aggravated the crisis by further embittering the peasants (though officially directed at the *kulaks*, in practice they struck at the peasants as a whole), and a chain reaction set in which seems to have played an important part in impelling Stalin to force a showdown. Another factor was that the apparatus of compulsion which he had concentrated in rural areas to secure grain in 1928–9 was available for an escalation of the struggle against the peasants.

Stalin told a meeting of Marxist agricultural experts on December 27, 1929, that 'we have moved on from a policy of *limiting* the exploiting tendencies of the *kulaks* to a policy of *liquidating* the *kulaks* as a class'.[19] (Stalin's emphasis.) And on January 5, 1930, the Communist Party of the Soviet Union (CPSU) Central Committee decreed 'that within the Five Year Plan period [i.e. by the end of 1933], instead of the collectivisation of 20 per cent of the sown area as laid down in the Plan, we can solve the problem of collectivising the vast majority of peasant households; and morever, the collectivisation of such important grain-growing areas as the Lower Volga, Middle Volga and North Caucasus can be basically completed by the autumn of 1930 or at any rate by the spring of 1931'.[20] The relatively sober collectivisation proposals adopted as recently as April 1929 were thus jettisoned, and the signal given for a headlong rush.

Thus was launched what was known as 'the policy of the liquidation of the *kulaks* as a class on the basis of wholesale collectivisation'—a policy which probably had more far-reaching consequences for the Soviet régime and people than any other initiated by Stalin.

COLLECTIVISATION, FIRST PHASE

A Politburo decree of January 30, 1930, 'on measures for the liquidation of *kulak* households in areas of wholesale collectivisation'[21] divided the *kulaks* into three groups. The first category was composed of 'the counter-revolutionary *aktiv*, the organisers of terrorist acts and of insurgent organisations'; the second of 'the remainder of the counter-revolutionary *aktiv*, composed of richer *kulaks* and semi-landowners'; and the third of 'all other *kulak* elements'.

The first category was to be arrested by the OGPU[22] (political police) and 'immediately isolated by being confined in corrective labour camps, while not hesitating to apply the highest measure of punishment [i.e. death] to organisers of terrorist acts, counter-revolutionary actions and insurgent organisations'.[23] The second category, like the first, was to be 'deported to remote localities of the USSR'.[24] The third was to be resettled locally, outside *kolkhoz* territory, on the worst land, such as 'eroded' areas, 'swamplands in woods' and other soil 'in need of improvement'.[25] In practice, however, the third category was treated no more leniently than the first two, for 'this category of *kulaks*, too, carried out an active struggle against the *kolkhozes* [and] the necessity arose to resettle it,

[19]

also, in the remoter areas'.[26] The deportation of the first two categories was to be carried out 'during February–May [1930], depending on the tempos of collectivisation in particular *oblasts* (regions), and with the aim of isolating not less than 50 per cent of the total by the beginning of sowing' [April 15].[27]

A decree of February 1, 1930, authorised the executive committee of local Soviets 'to apply all necessary measures of struggle with the *kulaks*, including the total confiscation of the *kulaks'* property and their deportation from the territory of particular *raions* and *krais* or *oblasts'*. The confiscated property 'must be transferred to the indivisible funds of *kolkhozes'*.[28] A supplementary decree of February 3 instructed the OGPU, in conjunction with the Russian Soviet Federative Socialist Republic (RSFSR) *Sovnarkom* (Council of the People's Commissars), to submit proposals 'for the resettlement of the *kulaks* and their families deported to remote localities of the RSFSR, and for their employment in work'.[29]

The brunt of the task of carrying out collectivisation and 'dekulakisation' fell on the OGPU. Operations at the local (*raion* and *okrug*) level were in the hands of specially formed *troikas* (three-man commissions) consisting of the First Secretary of the Party Committee, the chairman of the Soviet executive committee, and an OGPU representative.[30] 'Dekulakisation brigades' were formed of selected activists, and before the end of 1929 a first contingent of 25,000 industrial workers had been ordered by the All-Union Central Council of Trade Unions to reinforce them.[31]

An extensive purge of local party and Soviet officials was initiated before collectivisation to ensure, among other things, the removal of elements even slightly sympathetic to the peasants. The scale of the party purge may be judged by data for the important Central Black Earth *oblast*, where 5,322 members of the party organisation—13·4 per cent of its membership—were expelled, and 'several party *raikoms* (*raion* party committees) were disbanded for Rightist opportunism and certain *raikom* party secretaries were dismissed'.[32] The Soviets were ordered by a decree of January 31, 1930, to hold 'early re-elections of rural Soviets and *raion* executive committees'. The aim was 'the re-election of those village Soviets which were impregnated with alien elements . . . and of those *raion* executive committees which failed to direct the village Soviets or to start work on the collectivisation of agriculture'.

These measures were the prelude to Stalin's first great application of violence on a national scale, in which the whole apparatus of coercion and of the party cadres was engaged in a virtual civil war against the peasants. As a result, the Soviet State suffered a trauma as great as that left by the civil war, or, subsequently, by the *Ezhovshchina* (the Great Purge of the 1930s).

Very little of what happened has been revealed by official sources. The frankest admissions came as a by-product of Khrushchev's destalinisation of Soviet history, and the post-Khrushchev régime is now trying to disown these admissions.[33] Some idea of the violence, destruction and chaos which submerged the Soviet countryside in the early months of 1930 can, however, be gained from the account by Danilov, the foremost Khrushchevian historian of collectivisation:

'The mistakes and deviations made during the winter of 1929–30 caused enormous harm to the whole cause of mass collectivisation, aroused the discontent of the masses of poor and middle peasants and prepared the ground for provocations by enemies of the Soviet régime. In many places, anti-Soviet revolts were organised by the *kulaks*. Cases of bestial violence against Communists and *kolkhoz* activists became more frequent. The mass destruction of cattle began. As a result of deviations in *kolkhoz* construction and the hostile activities of the *kulaks* during the collectivisation years [from 1928 to 1933] 26·6 million head of cattle were destroyed (42·6 per cent), 15·3 million horses (47 per cent), 63·4 million sheep (65·1 per cent), etc. Livestock farming was dealt a heavy blow.[34] The *kolkhoz* movement, as a result of the mistakes, was on the verge of being discredited. A threat of disruption developed to the alliance of the working class and the peasantry, a threat to the very existence of the dictatorship of the proletariat. In the second half of February, 1930, the discontent of the peasant masses became exceptionally acute. The party Central Committee had to take decisive steps without delay to rectify the situation.'[35]

The 'mistakes and deviations' referred to by Danilov, and of which he gives detailed examples, were of four basic kinds, the common denominator being the indiscriminate use of violence and coercion:

(a) forcing peasants into collective farms by threatening to treat them as *kulaks* (i.e. to arrest and deport them and confiscate their property) and by other threats (e.g. to cut off all supplies, impose higher taxes);

(*b*) applying dekulakisation measures to all and sundry ('In some areas up to 15 per cent of peasant households were dekulakised. Among them were not only middle but even poor peasants'[36]);

(*c*) setting up instant collective farms by edict, without any consultation with the peasants concerned ('The organisation of *kolkhozes* was often carried out *en masse*, and the *kolkhozniks* had no clear idea of the objects and tasks of the *kolkhoz*.'[37]);

(*d*) forcing on the peasants an excessive degree of socialisation ('Communes were forcibly established. Also, in the establishing of *kolkhozes*, attempts were made to socialise all the cattle, which aroused the peasants' sharp discontent. *Krai* and *oblast* party committees vainly tried to get Stalin to explain the question of socialisation. There was no explanation.'[38])

PEASANT RESISTANCE

In the period leading up to mass collectivisation, peasant resistance, especially to grain procurements, was increasing. The rise of this resistance may be gauged by data for the Ukraine, where 'in the first half of 1928, 117 terrorist acts were registered. In the second half of 1928 and in 1929 *kulak* terror increased still further. From October, 1928, to February, 1929, the *kulaks* carried out 300 murders, woundings and acts of arson ... In 1929, the number of terrorist acts by *kulaks* rose four times compared with 1927.'[39]

For the peasant, the idea of entering a collective farm, even without compulsion, was abhorrent. It meant handing over whatever land, animals, implements, seed reserves, fodder, agricultural buildings and other equipment he may have possessed to a collective unit about which he had heard many unpleasant stories, from which he could not withdraw, over which he would have no control and the future of which seemed uncertain. Once mass collectivisation had begun, he had no alternative form of resistance to it except violence. And violence bred violence.

Official sources give only piecemeal data on the extent of the violence and blame it entirely on the *kulaks*:

'From agitating against the *kolkhozes* the *kulaks* turned to terror and sabotage. They murdered party and Soviet officials and *kolkhoz* organisers, set fire to *kolkhozes* and *kolkhoz* property, poisoned *kolkhoz* livestock and destroyed crops. *Kulak* aggressiveness increased from month to month ... The *kulaks'* desperate struggle against the *kolkhozes*, the establishment of counter-revolutionary insurgent organisations, and active resistance to collectivisation made it necessary to suppress *kulak* resistance and forcibly expropriate *kulak* means of production. The method of dekulakisation was forced on the Soviet régime, the working class and the working peasantry by the *kulaks* themselves, by their desperate resistance to the *kolkhoz* movement.'[40]

In the vital central Black Earth *oblast*, anti-Soviet mass demonstrations 'bore a semi-insurrectionary character ... people armed themselves with pitchforks, axes, staves, shot-guns, and hunting rifles ... In many cases they were headed by former Antonov [see p. 16] bandits'.[41]

In some non-Russian parts of the Soviet Union, notably Central Asia, resistance to collectivisation merged with local national resistance movements and became particularly acute. The population was almost united in regarding it as a threat to its national identity and way of life.

In Uzbekistan: 'the *kulak-bey* elements, supported in every way by bourgeois-nationalists, the reactionary [Muslim] clergy and other anti-Soviet elements, put up a stubborn resistance to the Socialist onslaught, and did not hesitate to use any means and methods of struggle ... In the cotton regions of Uzbekistan, the *kulaks'* resistance to collectivisation took on the character of widespread agitation for the reduction of cotton crops and an increase in wheat ... In some areas, the *kulaks* and *beys* organised several actions which were accompanied by the murder of active officials and *dekhans* [poor peasants]. In 1930, 333 terrorist acts were registered ... In connexion with mass collectivisation, certain Basmachi [a national resistance movement] gangs renewed their activity ... In 1930, in Uzbekistan, 16 bands were active[42]...'

In Kazakhstan, 'the *beys* organised migrations into remote steppe regions and even over the frontier of the USSR [i.e. into Sinkiang, China]'.[43]

In Kirgizia, resistance took the form of 'mass destruction of cattle and migration abroad. Under the influence of the *beys*, part of the population of the *auls* [villages] of Tuyuk and

Bogchata in the frontier Atbashinsk *raion* migrated to China, driving with them 30,000 sheep and 15,000 head of cattle. In the frontier regions of the Issyk-Kul, Tyan-Shan and Osh *okrugs* the *beys* and *manapas* [feudal aristocrats] formed bands which attacked *kolkhozes*.'[44]

In Turkmenistan: 'In many areas, the *beys* persuaded the peasants not to enter the *kolkhozes*, but to flee abroad, to slaughter cattle and destroy crops . . . In certain areas near the deserts, the Basmachi movement, which had almost been liquidated in the preceding years, intensified again. A tense political situation developed in the Republic.'[45]

The speed at which collectivisation was carried out in the winter of 1929–30 is an indication of its ferocity. Between October and March over half of all Soviet peasant families were collectivised.[46]

COLLECTIVISATION, SECOND PHASE

Even Stalin and his supporters must have been scared by the violence and chaos which their call for 'mass collectivisation' unleashed in a mere few weeks. It was imperative to call a halt before matters got completely out of hand. This Stalin did in his article, 'Dizziness from Successes', in *Pravda* of March 2, 1930. In it he tried to evade responsibility for the mistaken policy by alleging it had been 'distorted' by over-zealous local officials who applied force instead of the 'voluntary principle,'[47] and even attempted to take credit for saving the country from the crisis which he himself had provoked.[48] There followed a Central Committee decree of March 14, 1930, 'on the struggle against distortions of the party line in the *kolkhoz* movement',[49] which condemned the use of force and ordered strict adherence to the 'voluntary principle'. The response was an exodus from the collective farms, which reduced the proportion of collectivised peasant families from over a half to under a quarter by August, 1930.[50] But, 'despite the considerable exit from the collective farms in the spring of 1930, the basic mass of peasant households were consolidated in the *kolkhozes*'[51] and the respite was only temporary. Pressure was gradually resumed and by June, 1931, more than half the peasants (13 million families) were again collectivised in 211,000 *kolkhozes*.[52]

The year 1932 saw the introduction of savage legislation

directed at the peasants. A decree of August 7, 'on the guarding of State property',[53] ordered that all collective farm property (such as cattle, standing crops and agricultural produce) should henceforth be considered State property, 'sacred and inviolable'. Those guilty of offences against such property were to be considered 'enemies of the people'. There were to be only two penalties for its theft: execution by shooting and, where there were extenuating circumstances, imprisonment for not less than ten years with total confiscation of private property. A second part of the decree ordered that *kulaks* who attempted to force *kolkhozniks* to leave their collective farms were to be sentenced to between five and ten years in a concentration camp. Failure to report these crimes to the authorities was also a punishable offence. Those sentenced under the terms of the decree were to be excluded from amnesties. Official interpretations of the decree later declared that it was also to apply to persons who rendered false *kolkhoz* accounts, sabotaged agricultural work, or 'wrecked' crops, and so on.[54]

During 1932, 20 per cent of all those convicted by courts in the Soviet Union were dealt with under this decree,[55] which Stalin, in January, 1933, described as 'the basis of revolutionary legality at the present moment'.[56] It was subsequently revealed that Stalin had written the decree himself.[57]

The decree provided legal cover for whatever terroristic reprisals were thought necessary to break peasant resistance to collectivisation. Examples of this were given by former prosecutor-general Vyshinsky during a tongue-in-cheek denunciation[58] of 'some local officials' who, he admitted, had greeted the decree as a signal 'to shoot or roll into concentration camps as many people as possible'. He told how death sentences had been imposed for the theft of two sheaves of corn or 2½ kilograms of flour, and recounted how one young man had been sent to a concentration camp for ten years for having 'frolicked in a barn with some girls at night, thus disturbing the *kolkhoz* pig'.

A fortnight later there followed a decree 'on the fight against speculation'.[59] Stalin remarked: 'This law does not suffer from particular mildness.'[60] It ordered 'the OGPU, the Prokuratura and the local authorities to take measures for the eradication of speculation' (which had been defined as the purchase and resale for profit by private citizens of agricultural products and goods of mass consumption), 'applying to speculators and dealers imprisonment in a concentration camp for between five and ten years without the right of amnesty'. It was later admitted that this decree, too, had been 'misinterpreted' and applied, for example, to kolkhozniks for attempting to sell the produce of their private plots.[61]

In December, 1932, an extensive internal passport system was introduced, ostensibly in order to expel 'kulaks, criminals and other anti-social elements'[62] from urban areas. All movement was strictly controlled, the system being administered by the OGPU's Chief Administration of Militia. Only urban dwellers were issued with passports and could move about the country if they registered their passports with the militia at each move. Non-passport-holders (in effect, collective farmers) were forbidden to live where passports were required (all urban and frontier areas) and could only pay short visits to their local towns in special circumstances.

Even more difficult than forcing the peasants into kolkhozes was getting the kolkhozes to function. The newly formed ones —where they did not exist merely on paper—seriously lacked experienced managers, equipment and machinery, and the working morale of the peasants could not have been lower. Stalin automatically attributed these difficulties to 'well-camouflaged anti-Soviet elements, who organise wrecking and sabotage' in the farms, and so justified a further round of terror.[63]

A Central Committee resolution of January 11, 1933,[64] read:

'Anti-Soviet elements, penetrating the kolkhozes in the capacity of accountants, managers, storekeepers, brigadiers and so on, and often in the capacity of leading officials of kolkhoz boards, are trying to organise wrecking, putting machines out of order, sowing badly, squandering kolkhoz property, undermining labour discipline, organising the theft of seeds, secret granaries and the sabotage of the grain harvest; and sometimes they succeed in breaking the kolkhozes up.'

The resolution demanded the expulsion of these 'anti-Soviet elements' from collective and State farms. It entrusted this task to newly-established 'political departments' in all Machine-Tractor Stations (MTS)* and State farms—in particular to their deputy heads, who were OGPU officials. The political departments were staffed by party officials specially selected by a Politburo commission,[65] and were ordered 'to ensure party

* See p. 38.

[26]

control and act as the party's eye in all spheres of the life and work of the MTS and State farms themselves, and of the *kolkhozes* served by the MTS'.

Since the rural *raion* party committees were weak and considered untrustworthy,[66] the MTS political departments were made independent of them and given exclusive authority to direct party and Komsomol work in the *kolkhozes*. The OGPU deputy heads ran their own 'agent-informer networks',[67] which supplied reports on hostile conversations and activities. These subsequently formed the basis for purges and arrests. In March, 1933, OGPU disclosures of 'subversive activities' in the Commissariat of Agriculture and State Farms resulted in 36 death sentences and 44 sentences of long-term imprisonment for Commissariat employees.[68]

By the spring of 1933, this new round of terror was as out of hand as the initial phase of collectivisation had been three years earlier, and once again Stalin intervened to call for 'moderation' and disclaim responsibility. A secret instruction[69] 'to all party and Soviet officials, organs of the OGPU, the judiciary and the Prokuratura', of May 8, 1933, which he signed together with Molotov (chairman of the *Sovnarkom*), said:

'The Central Committee and the *Sovarkom* are informed that disorderly mass arrests are still part of the practice of our officials . . . Arrests are made by all who so desire and who, strictly speaking, have no right to make arrests. It is not surprising that in such a saturnalia of arrests, organs which do have the right to arrest, including the OGPU and especially the militia, lose all feeling of moderation and often perpetrate arrests without any basis, acting according to the rule: "First arrest, and then investigate." '

The extent of the purge emerges from figures given by Danilov[70]:

'According to the data of the political departments of 24 *oblasts*, *krais* and Republics of the USSR, in 1933 over 30 per cent of agronomists were removed from their jobs, 47·3 per cent of managers, 34·3 per cent of storekeepers, 25 per cent of accountants, 23·7 per cent of clerks, 24·4 per cent of stablehands, and 13 per cent of tractor-drivers. The main grounds for this were accusations of wrecking. Between a quarter and a third of *kolkhoz* chairmen of Kazakhstan, Lower Volga and North Caucasus were declared enemies of the *kolkhoz* system. Ya. A. Yakovlev, at that time People's Commissar for Agriculture of the USSR, said at the beginning of 1935 that during the last two years, hundreds of thousands of *kolkhozniks* were expelled from the *kolkhozes*, but only a few of these were really incorrigible enemies of the *kolkhoz* system.'

THE COST OF COLLECTIVISATION

It is impossible to estimate the human cost of collectivisation in the early 1930s. The most that official sources admit is that 'from the beginning of 1930 until the autumn of 1932, 240,757 *kulak* families—i.e., about one per cent of the total number of peasant households—were deported from the areas of wholesale collectivisation'.[71] But there is plenty of official evidence that not only *kulaks*, but middle and poor peasants suffered under 'dekulakisation' measures. As collectivisation proceeded, other categories were discovered to be 'enemies of collectivisation' and to require the same form of repression as the *kulak*. These included such ill-defined groups as the *podkulachnik* (peasants sympathetic to the *kulaks*), and 'enemies of the people' (under the decree of August 7, 1932, referred to above). The term *kulak* itself was never legally defined, and no official criterion was ever agreed on for identifying members of this 'class' to be liquidated.[72] In practice, of course, it was a peasant's political attitude, especially towards collectivisation, not his social or economic standing, that determined how he was treated. It is also clear that not only relatively prosperous peasants resisted collectivisation, but in many areas the entire peasant population.

The Politburo commission charged with preparing for 'dekulakisation' in December, 1929, used an estimate of five to six million[73] for the number of persons in *kulak* families (this would correspond roughly with Stalin's estimate, a year earlier, that kulaks constituted five per cent of peasant families,[74] or more than a million of the 25 million peasant families). It would be reasonable to suppose that at least five to six million people were deported to Siberia and the far North, where many must have perished under the notorious slave labour system.

As a result of the disintegration of the peasant economy caused by collectivisation, the Soviet Union suffered in 1932-4 one of the worst famines ever. It was most severe in the grain-growing regions: the Ukraine, the North Caucasus (particularly the Kuban), the middle and lower Volga, and in Kazakhstan.

The most careful estimates of deaths from starvation are about five and a half million.[75] The Soviet authorities refused to admit the existence of the famine, tried to conceal it, refused all offers of foreign aid (unlike the time of the 1921–3 famine) and continued to export grain[76] in order to buy machinery for industrialisation. Indeed, there seems to have been more concern at the loss of livestock than of peasants, for Stalin had no scruples in waging a 'war of starvation'[77] against them. A particularly gruesome feature of the famine was cannibalism, of which several reports reached the outside world.[78] During the Khrushchev period a Soviet novel containing a description of the famine in the Ukraine hinted that this had occurred.[79] The Ukrainian population went down from 31 million in 1926 to 28 million in 1939.

The human cost of collectivisation was particularly heavy in Central Asia. In Kazakhstan, 'many mistakes made in 1930–1 ... led to an enormous destruction of productive forces and the death of many people in the *auls* [villages]', according to a Khrushchevite historian.[80] The Kazakh people, in fact, appear to have suffered a population loss of 1·5 million, attributable to collectivisation.[81] Several million nomads or semi-nomads were forced to settle, though many succeeded in migrating to China.[82]

In Uzbekistan, 'during 1930–3, 40,000 *bey* and *kulak* households were liquidated, constituting above five per cent of all peasant households. The majority of *kulaks* in Uzbekistan were resettled in other regions of the Soviet Union.'[83]

'The deportation of *beys* from the more advanced areas of the Turkmen SSR was carried out in August and November, 1930, when 1,943 dekulakised households were deported. The more vicious representatives of the *beys* were deported outside the Republic. In 1930 and 1931, a total of 2,211 *kulak* (*bey*) and landowner families were deported from the Republic.'[84]

For the régime, the imposition of the collective farm system had four principal advantages:

(a) It finally destroyed the peasants' power to hold the régime to ransom by withholding grain supplies, reducing sown areas, or forcing up prices.

(b) It made possible the extension into the countryside of detailed political control by the party and police, and of methods of labour organisation and discipline similar to those already developed in industry. Henceforth all those agricultural tasks which the peasants had performed automatically, such as sowing and ploughing, were the subject of official party campaigns and directives.

(c) It made it possible to control the level of the peasants' home consumption and thus ensure procurements of agricultural produce at terms and in quantities dictated by the régime, and

(d) It facilitated the mobilisation of rural labour resources for large-scale transfers to industry and for the colonisation of under-populated areas in Siberia and the Far East.

Already, by 1932, grain procurements by the State were more than twice those of 1927, before collectivisation, although the harvest was much smaller.[85]

On the other hand, agricultural production, especially livestock farming, suffered a severe blow, and the pre-collectivisation level of output was not reached again until about 1955.

CONSOLIDATION OF THE
COLLECTIVE FARM SYSTEM

By the end of 1934, three-quarters of the peasant households and nine-tenths of the sown area had been collectivised in 240,000 collective farms.[86] Peasant resistance had been broken by famine and terror, and the authorities began to concentrate on consolidating the new system. The main instrument for this was the revised 'Model Statutes'[87] for the collective farms, adopted by the second congress of *kolkhoznik*-shock-workers in February, 1935, in strict conformity with which statutes were adopted by the farms themselves during 1935 and 1936.

The main features of the statutes were:

(a) The *kolkhoz* undertook 'to conduct its collective economy according to the plan, adhering strictly to the plans for agricultural production established by the organs of the worker-peasant government and to its obligations to the State (Art. 6)';

(b) As the first charge on its production, it undertook 'to fulfil its obligations to the State for deliveries and for returning seed-loans, and paying the MTS in kind...' (Art. 11a); and, as the last priority, after fulfilling other obligations, such as building up seed- and fodder- reserves, 'it distributes all the remainder of the harvest and of the livestock products between the *kolkhoz* members . . .' (Art. 11d);

(c) Each peasant household was permitted to retain a small plot of land for its own use, limited to between a quarter and half a hectare (0·62 to 1·24 acres) and exceptionally, in some areas, one hectare (2·47 acres) and a small amount of private livestock, the standard allowance being: one cow, up to two head of young cattle, one sow with offspring, up to ten sheep and/or goats, unlimited poultry and rabbits, up to 20 beehives (Arts. 2, 5);

(d) 'The distribution of the *artel*'s [*kolkhoz*'s] income among members is carried out exclusively according to the number of labour-days* worked by each member' (Art. 15);

(e) The 'highest organ' of the *kolkhoz* was declared to be the general meeting of its members, which elected the chairman and a board of five to nine members to run its affairs in the intervals between general meetings (Arts. 20. 21);

(f) The *kolkhoz* undertook to consider theft of *kolkhoz* property and a 'wrecking attitude' as 'treachery to the common cause of the *kolkhoz* and aid to the enemies of the people' (see decree of August 7, 1932, referred to above), and to hand over those 'guilty of such criminal undermining of the bases of the *kolkhoz* system' to the courts, 'for the infliction of punishment according to the full severity of the laws of the worker-peasant government' (Art. 18).

(a) COMPULSORY DELIVERIES

For the authorities, the *kolkhoz* had one overriding function: to ensure that, no matter what happened, the State got its quota of each harvest and of animal products. Stalin declared, and the Soviet Press consistently repeated, that the fulfilment of compulsory deliveries was 'the first commandment of workers of Socialist agriculture' and 'the most important economic and political task of all local party and Soviet organisations".[88]

A decree of January 19, 1933, 'on compulsory deliveries of grain to the State by *kolkhozes* and individual peasant farms',[89]

* *See* p. 36.

[31]

substituted for the hitherto largely arbitrary assessments made in the guise of 'contracts', a new system of obligatory deliveries 'having the force of a tax', based on the farms' planned sown areas, and paid for at very low fixed State prices. According to the decree, fulfilment of these deliveries 'is the prior duty of every *kolkhoz* and individual peasant farm, and the first grain threshed must be used for carrying this out'. It permitted the farms to sell grain on *kolkhoz* markets[90] only after fulfilment of the grain deliveries plan by the whole Republic, *krai* and *oblast* . . . and the complete replenishing of the seed funds'. Farms failing to complete their deliveries according to a fixed proportion of the total in each harvest month received proportionate monetary fines and were ordered to fulfil their entire annual deliveries ahead of schedule (Arts. 15, 16).

The system for the obligatory delivery of meat, milk, butter, cheese, wool, etc., was altered in the same way as that for grain by decrees issued on September 23 and December 19, 1932, and based on the supposed number of animals on a farm at a given time.[91]

The progress of obligatory deliveries of agricultural products to the State was supervised by a Committee for Deliveries of Agricultural Products attached to the USSR *Sovnarkom*, with nationwide representation at all administrative levels down to the *raion*.[92] The committee's *raion* representative was 'personally responsible for ensuring by all means the exaction genuinely ahead of schedule of the entire unfulfilled portion of the planned annual grain deliveries from *kolkhozes*' and, on the basis of monthly checks, instructed the local Soviets to impose fines on laggard *kolkhozes*.

The State exacted grain deliveries from the farms not only in the form of compulsory deliveries at 'symbolic'[93] prices, but also in the form of payments in kind made by the farms to the MTS for work done on their fields. In the late 1930s, the State obtained slightly more grain by this second method than by the first.[94] It was introduced by a decree of February 5, 1933, which established that the MTS should receive 20 per cent of the grain harvest in return for performing 'all the basic agricultural work on the fields of the *kolkhoz*'.[95] A decree of June 25, 1933, said that legal proceedings would be started against any *kolkhoz* trying to avoid these payments in kind to the MTS.[96]

Yet another channel for compulsory grain deliveries was the exorbitant payments in kind for the grinding of grain exacted from *kolkhozes* and *kolkhozniks*. It was not until 1954 that cash payments were finally substituted for these payments in kind.[97]

Obligatory deliveries were also exacted from the small private plots of *kolkhoz* peasant households. They were based on the same system that applied to the *kolkhozes* but were generally at lower rates.[98] *Kolkhoz* households were, however, obliged to deliver meat and potatoes, even though they had no livestock and grew no potatoes.[99]

Kolkhoz deliveries to the State and payments in kind to the MTS are thought to have amounted to 26 per cent of the grain harvest in 1937, 31 per cent in 1938 and 34 per cent in 1939. During 1935–7, an average of 68 per cent of the meat and animal fats, 45 per cent of the milk, and 53 per cent of the wool produced collectively is believed to have gone to the State.[100] No statistics are available for subsequent years, but the proportion of deliveries is thought to have been larger, because after 1940[101] deliveries were based on the arable or total *kolkhoz* area, instead of on the planned sown area and number of livestock.

Having delivered their compulsory quotas, *kolkhozes* and *kolkhozniks*, under a system introduced in 1932, were under pressure to sell grain and other products to the State at prices higher than quota prices but still well below *kolkhoz* market prices. There was a large element of compulsion in these 'voluntary' sales, but they carried the privilege of buying scarce manufactured goods at State retail prices and so had some attraction even for farms with access to a *kolkhoz* market.[102]

(b) PRIVATE PLOTS AND LIVESTOCK

The right of each *kolkhoznik* household to maintain and cultivate a small private plot of land, and to rear a small number of private livestock, was solemnly embodied in Article 7 of the USSR's 'Stalin' Constitution of 1936. But Stalin regarded this as a temporary concession, which could be withdrawn gradually once the *kolkhoz* system had become firmly established. He explained to the *Kolkhoznik* congress which adopted the Model Statutes in February, 1935:

'Under present conditions, you must take into account the *kolkhozniks'* private interests as well as their general interests . . . It is best to admit directly, frankly and honestly that a *kolkhoz* household must have its own private plot, a small one, but its own . . . Otherwise it is impossible to strengthen the *kolkhozes*. To combine the private interests of the *kolkhozniks* with the communal interests of the *kolkhozes*—therein lies the key to strengthening the *kolkhozes*.[103]

The officially permitted holdings of private livestock, though limited, were higher than many *kolkhozniks* ever achieved. By 1938, even though 55·7 per cent of the country's cows were privately owned by *kolkhozniks*,[104] this meant that there were only 12·1 million cows in a total of 18·5 million households.[105] Although no limitations were imposed on poultry and rabbits, these animals were relatively rare. More important was the total prohibition, except in some nomadic areas, on the private ownership of horses. The peasants, who had formerly relied on horses for a variety of tasks, could now only use one with the authority of the *kolkhoz* board, and on payment (Article 4 of the Model Statutes).

These statutes suggested that the private plots would be used merely as 'kitchen gardens and orchards'. But for most *kolkhozniks* the plot, tiny as it was, represented the last remnant of their traditional way of life and a more rewarding focus of activity than the collective farm itself. Despite difficulties such as lack of equipment, fodder and fertiliser, the *kolkhoznik* managed to secure a surprisingly large return from this land. In 1938 the private plots were responsible for no less than 21·5 per cent of total Soviet agricultural produce, although they covered only 3·8 per cent of the cultivated land.[106] Thus, even though the peasants had been forced into the collective farms, the battle for collectivisation had not been concluded. By the beginning of the Second World War, the *kolkhoznik's* private plot was still his main source of income.[107] Far from reconciling private and collective interests by tolerating this residue of private farming, the *kolkhoz* system perpetuated and fostered competition and conflict between them.

At the Communist Party of the Soviet Union's 18th congress in 1939 Andreev, a Politburo member in charge of agriculture, admitted that 'in some places, the private plot economy of the *kolkhoz* household has begun to outgrow the communal economy of the *kolkhoz*, and is becoming the basic economy, while the *kolkhoz* economy, on the other hand, is becoming the subsidiary one'.[108] He claimed that private plots were no longer necessary because the *kolkhozes* were strong enough to supply all the needs of the *kolkhozniks*, and insisted that 'the private economy of *kolkhoz* households must increasingly take on a strictly subordinate character while the communal-*kolkhoz* economy grows as the basic one".[109]

Soon after the CPSU congress, stern measures were introduced to enforce this policy and restrict the growth of the private plots and the amount of time spent on them. A decree of May 27, 1939,[110] said that the plots were being illegally extended at the expense of *kolkhoz* land, and 'to the advantage of private property and self-seeking elements who make use of the *kolkhoz* for speculation and private profit.' It complained that the plots were treated as 'private property ... which the *kolkhoznik*, and not the *kolkhoz*, disposes of at his own discretion', and that they were even leased out to other peasants. It also said that 'there is a fairly considerable proportion of pseudo-*kolkhozniks* who either do not work at all in the *kolkhozes*, or work only for show, spending most of their time on their private plot'.

The decree provided for the following measures:

(a) All attempts to extend private plots above the statutory limits or to encroach on collective farm land to be dealt with as criminal acts, and all local party and Soviet officials permitting such acts to be expelled from their posts and the party and to be prosecuted.

(b) *Kolkhozniks* who lease their private plots to be expelled from the *kolkhoz* and deprived of their plots.

(c) A survey of all private plots to be carried out by August 15, 1939, and all surplus land discovered on them to be taken over by the *kolkhozes* by November 15, 1939[111]; the boundaries between plots and *kolkhoz* land to be clearly marked with posts; a permanent corps of inspectors to carry out further periodic surveys; surveyors carrying out inaccurate measurements to be dealt with by the courts.[112]

(d) Every able-bodied *kolkhoznik*, including women, to work a minimum number of labour-days each year on the *kolkhoz* (100 in cotton-growing areas, 80 in most other agricultural areas, 60 in areas with short growing seasons), or face expulsion from the *kolkhoz*.

(e) A Resettlement Administration to be established for organising the transfer of *kolkhozniks* to areas such as

Kazakhstan and the Far East, ostensibly from areas of land shortage to where it was plentiful, because 'reserves of land for assignment to the *kolkhozniks* as private plots according to the statutory norms have already been exhausted in *kolkhozes* where land is short.'

(c) ORGANISATION OF
WORK ON COLLECTIVE FARMS

At an early stage of collectivisation, it was recognised that

'The most important and most harmful mistakes in the work of the *kolkhozes* in 1930 were, firstly, the distribution of *kolkhoz* income on a *per capita* basis instead of according to the quantity and quality of the *kolkhoznik*'s work; and, secondly, inept and bad organisation of labour.'[113]

The recommended remedy for the first of these mistakes was:

'The distribution of *kolkhoz* incomes according to the principle that those who work more and better receive more; those who do not work receive nothing. In conformity with this piecework, calculated in labour-days, is to be applied on a large scale in the basic agricultural operations such as ploughing, sowing, weeding, harvesting and threshing.'[114]

The 'labour-day' is an artificial accounting unit for crediting *kolkhozniks* for their work on the *kolkhoz*, having the value of a dividend in the *kolkhoz*'s disposable income (in cash and in agricultural produce, mainly grain), which can only be calculated at the end of each agricultural year, after the *kolkhoz* has met all its other commitments. More, or less, than one labour-day can be credited for an actual day's work, depending on the nature of that work.

A decree of February 28, 1933, 'on the value in labour-days of various agricultural operations in the *kolkhozes* and on model work-norms for 1933', divided *kolkhoz* workers into seven groups.[115] The seventh, or top, group, which was to be paid two labour-days for a day's work, included chairmen of large *kolkhozes* and operators of complex machinery including senior tractor drivers. The first, or bottom, group, to be paid half a labour-day for a day's work, included guards, messengers and cleaners.

'Work-norms accessible to a conscientiously working *kolkhoznik*' were established, in accordance with Article 15 of the Model Statutes, for every task (in terms, for example, of ploughing one hectare of land or threshing one ton of grain) and *kolkhozniks* were credited with labour-day units on condition that they fulfilled the corresponding work-norm. At least once a week, the 'brigadier' entered the number of labour-days which he calculated had been earned by a *kolkhoznik* in the latter's 'work-book' (Art. 15). Provision was made for small advances of cash and grain to be made to *kolkhozniks*, proportionate to their labour-day earnings (Art. 16).

The labour-day payment system was subsequently developed and refined under pressure from Stalin to liquidate wage-levelling (*uravnilovka*) and to provide better incentives. Thus various premia, in extra labour-days, could be won for good quality work, etc.; and regional variations were taken into account. The payment of *kolkhoz* chairmen and other administrative staff was subsequently (in 1940) altered, and based on a fixed number of labour-days per year,[116] according to the size of the farm.

The actual value of the labour-day during the 1930s, in terms of the cash and agricultural produce distributed to the *kolkhozniks* for their labour-days, was extremely low and quite insufficient to cover their minimum needs. In 1938, it appears that they received from this source only about three-quarters of their grain requirements, less than half their food potatoes and negligible amounts of other foodstuffs. Their cash receipts amounted to only about 20 per cent of their total cash receipts from all sources.[117] Generally, the cash element in payment for labour-days was slight and often non-existent; the most important element was grain.

A decree of April 19, 1938, admitted: 'In some *oblasts* and Republics ... there are *kolkhozes* in which the cash income in 1937 was not distributed at all for labour-days.' This was blamed on 'enemies of the people ... [who] for provocative purposes—to undermine the *kolkhozes*—deliberately inspired the artificial inflation of their capital and production costs and the reduction of monetary income distributed for labour-days.' The decree ordered that not less than 60–70 per cent of a *kolkhoz*'s monetary income should be distributed for labour-days, and that capital expenditure should not exceed 10 per cent of this income.[118] This ruling was, however, rescinded in December of the same year.[119]

A solution to the labour organisation problem in the *kolkhozes* was first sought by dividing the *kolkhozniks* into groups of up to 100 called 'brigades', under a 'brigadier'. A decree of February 4, 1932, said that the brigades should be 'the most important unit in the organisation of labour in *kolkhozes*', and that they should carry out all the basic agricultural tasks on the sector of the farm assigned to them,[120] as well as being responsible for the machinery, tools and draught animals necessary for the cultivation of their sector. The labour-days awarded to the *kolkhozniks* would depend on the success of the brigade as a whole.

This idea was developed in the Collective Farm Model Statutes of 1935, Article 14 of which extended the period for which a brigade was assigned to a particular sector to not less than a full crop rotation. It also provided for 'livestock brigades' formed for periods of not less than three years. The brigadiers were instructed, 'in distributing work, not to show any kind of favouritism or clannishness'.

It soon became clear, however, that a smaller unit was needed, especially for the cultivation of crops such as potatoes and vegetables, and the authorities increasingly favoured the 'link' or 'squad' (*zveno*) of six to 12 people, headed by a 'linkman' (*zvenevoi*), for which no provision had been made in the Model Statutes.

The principle of encouraging individual responsibility for particular tasks, especially through the *zveno* system, and consequently of temporarily parcelling out *kolkhoz* land and livestock to small groups, individual households or even to individual *kolkhozniks*, was officially endorsed at the CPSU's 18th congress in 1939, at which Andreev said:

'The more labour is individualised in the *kolkhozes* through the links or individual *kolkhozniks*, and the more their labour is given material incentives, the more productive it is . . . The experience of the link organisation of labour has justified itself not only for technical crops. Quite a lot of *kolkhozes* have gone over to the establishment of links in the field-cultivating, grain brigades as well . . . We must proceed more decisively towards the link organisation of labour in the *kolkhozes* and brigades.'[121]

(d) THE MTS (MACHINE-TRACTOR STATION)

As well as acting as the main instrument for imposing party controls over the countryside and as a procurement agency for ensuring deliveries of produce to the State, the MTS exerted close operational control over the *kolkhozes* by virtue of their monopoly of mechanical power.

MTS started operating in 1930, when mass collectivisation was already under way. They were based on the principle that maximum use could be obtained from equipment by pooling it and were inaugurated by a decree of June 5, 1929,[122] which ordered a network of stations to be established covering not less than a million hectares. Almost 2,500 MTS were established between 1929 and 1932,[123] and by 1940 there were more than 7,000.[124] Each served several *kolkhozes*.

Originally, it was envisaged that the MTS would be co-operative undertakings belonging to the *kolkhozes* and financed by them jointly with the State. The June, 1929, decree which established for this purpose as controlling body a joint stock organisation—the 'All-Union Centre of Machine Tractor Stations' (*Tractorotsentr*)—said that it was 'absolutely essential to absorb, in addition to State and co-operative funds assigned for creating MTS, the funds of the peasant population served by these stations'. At the end of 1932, however, *Tractorotsentr* was reorganised, and control of the MTS, which became entirely State organisations, passed to the People's Commissariat of Agriculture.[125]

Relations between the *kolkhozes* and the MTS were regulated by annual 'contracts' which authorised the MTS to interfere in practically every sphere of *kolkhoz* life, placed it in charge of all major agricultural tasks and obliged the *kolkhozes* to carry out MTS instructions to the smallest detail. The Model Contract for 1934,[126] for example, declared:

'The MTS undertakes constantly to help the *kolkhoz* to strengthen itself economically and organisationally by providing it with agronomical services, drawing up its production and finance plans; establishing correct crop-rotations; assisting in the organisation of labour and distribution of income, in the training of cadres and in the organisation of accounting. All operations in the fields, including work with tractors, are carried out by the *kolkhozniks* themselves, according to the procedure laid down by the MTS in agreement with the *kolkhoz*.'

The MTS Director, senior agronomist, chief mechanic and chief book-keeper were appointed by the Commissariat of Agriculture.[127] The operational units were tractor brigades, headed by a brigadier and with several tractors and drivers on its strength. The brigadiers and tractor-drivers were appointed by the MTS Director from among *kolkhozniks* who had trained and qualified at special MTS schools.[128] They remained members of their *kolkoz*, though as tractor-drivers they were under the direction of the MTS, and had to work on all the *kolkhozes* which it serviced. They were paid in labour-days, but at considerably higher rates than the ordinary *kolkhozniks*, and they were subject to special schemes of incentives and penalties (e.g. for economising or wasting fuel). They were also privileged by being guaranteed a minimum payment in cash and kind for their labour-days (2·5 roubles and 3 kilos of grain).[129]

THE PURGES

The Great Purge of 1936–8, during which countless people in all walks of life fell victim to Stalin's witch-hunt, though it struck hardest at the urban population, did not leave the countryside unscathed. Some idea of the terror which spread to rural areas may be gained from Andreev's speech at the 18th party congress in 1939:

'We must not underestimate the fact that enemies of the people of all sorts undoubtedly caused much harm to the collective and State farms by wrecking in agriculture. It is now clear that enemies of the people under the direction of foreign intelligence prepared and carried out a plan for widespread provocation. All methods were employed in order to create famine in the *kolkhoz* village, and to arouse discontent in the country ... Wreckers in disguise carried out the mass infecting of *kolkhoz* and *sovkhoz* cattle with glanders, Siberian plague and other infectious diseases, and through the cattle they also infected people ... In order to undermine the *kolkhozes*, enemies infiltrated the agricultural departments and destroyed agricultural machinery in MTS and *sovkhozes*. They carried out shallow ploughing in the fields in order to infest the grain crops with weeds, hindered the grain harvest in every way, spoiled the grain while it was still standing, made the harvested grain rot in the barns and infected it with ticks ... Agriculture was evidently the main target for the enemy's wrecking and sabotage.'[130]

The purge also served to provide scapegoats for agricultural failures. For example, the infection of crops with ticks in 1937 was blamed by Vyshinsky on 'counter-revolutionary elements', on whom 'severe measures of punishment' were inflicted, though it has recently been admitted that this was 'totally without foundation'. The 'agricultural wrecking' to which several of the accused at the Bukharin trial in March, 1938, confessed are a good indication of the failures which it was felt necessary to try and explain away. The most prominent victim was M. A. Chernov, People's Commissar for Agriculture, who was held responsible for sabotaging the food supply, and was shot.[131] (The first three USSR Commissars of Agriculture, Ya. A. Yakovlev (December, 1929–May, 1934), Chernov (May, 1934–October, 1937) and R. I. Eikhe (October, 1937–April, 1938), all perished in the purges.)

SECOND WORLD WAR
AND POST-WAR RECONSTRUCTION

During the Second World War, 47 per cent of the pre-war sown area and 45 per cent of the pre-war livestock herds came under enemy occupation; most of this livestock was slaughtered or removed by the Germans. The area overrun included the richest agricultural areas—the Ukraine and North Caucasus—and little could be done to offset this loss by expanding sown areas in non-occupied territory in the East. According to official estimates, 98,000 *kolkhozes,* 1,876 *sovkhozes* and 2,890 MTS were wholly or partially destroyed.[132]

In the occupied areas, the peasants' hopes that the Germans might disband the *kolkhozes* and restore private farming were not usually fulfilled; the invaders found the *kolkhozes* useful as food-gathering points. In the non-occupied areas the farms were denuded of able-bodied men, and almost devoid of machinery, horses and implements. What work was done was performed by women[133] and children, and occasionally by workers mobilised from nearby towns. In an effort to extract the maximum effort from the remaining *kolkhozniks* a decree of April 13, 1942,[134] raised their minimum annual compulsory labour-days for the three zones[135] to 150, 120 and 100. It also established the minimum number of labour-days to be earned in each agricultural season. The penalty for non-fulfilment was six months' corrective labour on the *kolkhoz.*

Wartime conditions, especially the acute food shortages, heightened the importance of the *kolkhozniks'* private plots and provided scope for widespread evasion or disregard of restrictions on them. Moreover, it was apparently widely expected that a relaxation of the collective farm system would come with the end of the war.[136] These hopes were dashed:

[41]

restoration of the system in its most rigorous form was the main aim of post-war policy.

A decree of September 19, 1946, 'on measures for the liquidation of violations of the *kolkhoz* Charter',[137] was, in essence, a repetition of the draconian decree of May 27, 1939 (see p. 35) which, it was admitted, had been 'forgotten by many officials'. Once again the illegal extension of private plots and dispersal of collective land and property was the chief target for denunciation. But also under attack was the swollen farm bureaucracy which was blamed for 'infringements of *kolkhoz* democracy', and for the low value of labour-day payments to *kolkhozniks*. Once again, a survey of private plots and *kolkhoz* land was ordered so that estranged *kolkhoz* land could be returned. A Council for *Kolkhoz* Affairs (presided over by Andreev) was established to enforce discipline. As a result of its activities, 14 million acres were restored to the *kolkhozes*,[138] and more than 500,000 farm bureaucrats or non-production personnel were transferred to production, and 213,000 people without real connection with the *kolkhozes* were removed from the payrolls.[139] A decree of September 14, 1948, however, said that the reduction of administrative personnel had not gone far enough and urged further drastic cuts.[140]

An important aspect of the post-war reassertion of controls was the reactivation of the MTS and an attempt to expand MTS and *kolkhoz* party organisations. The February, 1947, Central Committee plenum decided to reinstitute the post of 'MTS Deputy for political work', which had been created in 1934[141] but later (probably during the war) fell into abeyance. His tasks included 'to ensure correct relations between the MTS and the *kolkhozes*, guard over the strict adherence of *kolkhozes* and the MTS to their contractual relations, so that there is no mutual concealment of mistakes . . . and improve the work of the MTS party organisations'.[142]

Work-norms and the pay and incentives structure were tightened up by a decree of April 19, 1948.[143] It introduced new, tougher work-norms and ordered them to be revised annually in order not to lag behind 'the attained level of productivity'. Pay differentials were increased on the basis that '*kolkhozniks* of brigades and links achieving bigger harvests should receive higher pay and . . . [those] achieving lower harvests should receive lower pay'.

The campaign to discourage *kolkhozniks* from spending time

on their private plots was strengthened in 1948 by a large increase in the agricultural tax levied on income from these plots, and by further increases in 1950 and 1951.

After the war the *kolkhoz* system was extended to the three Baltic States of Lithuania, Latvia and Estonia; to Moldavia, and to the newly acquired Western districts of the Ukraine and Belorussia. Collectivisation was largely accomplished between 1948 and 1950, and with the same violence and terror which had characterised this step elsewhere in the early 1930s. In Estonia, for example, 'mass collectivisation proceeded in conditions of a sharp aggravation of the class struggle. Hostile elements stopped at nothing. They slandered the *kolkhozes* and the *kolkhozniks*, and tried by threats, provocations and murders to terrorize the *kolkhozniks* ... [and] placed the Soviet Government under the necessity of depriving the *kulaks* of their implements and means of production and transferring their land and equipment to the *kolkhozes*'.[144] MTS political departments were set up in the newly collectivised areas where they existed from January, 1951, to January, 1954, to ensure political discipline.[145]

The difficulties of the early post-war years were aggravated by famine and drought. The 1946 drought was officially stated to be worse than that of 1921.[146] The Soviet Union was aided after the Second World War, as after the first, by the United States, which supplied foodstuffs through UNRA until 1946.[147] But Stalin reacted to the situation just as he had done to the famine of 1932–4. Khrushchev later revealed:

'The method [Stalin's and Molotov's] was like this: they sold grain abroad, while in some regions people were swollen with hunger and even dying from lack of bread. Yes, comrades, it is a fact that in 1947 in many of the country's *oblasts*, for example in the Kursk *oblast*, people were dying from hunger. But grain was at this time being exported!'[148]

In the last few years of Stalin's rule, 1950–3, agricultural questions became a centre of controversy within the party leadership. The disputes grew intense enough to gain public expression and crucially affected several members of the leadership.[149]

The first issue in dispute, the organisation of labour in the *kolkhozes*, came into the open with a sudden attack on Andreev in *Pravda* on February 19, 1950, for advocating the link system in preference to the brigade. Although links had been officially encouraged, not only by Andreev, since before the war, they now became an object of suspicion, and Andreev lost his position as Politburo spokesman on agriculture. (The implications of this episode are dealt with in section III, since the links controversy re-emerged, with considerable significance, under the Brezhnev–Kosygin régime.)

The second issue concerned the amalgamation of the *kolkhozes*. On March 8, 1950, only a few weeks after the rebuke to Andreev, *Pravda* published a speech by Khrushchev in which he outlined the advantages of merging *kolkhozes*, arguing that this would give them access to greater resources of machinery and expertise and improve their efficiency. He claimed that the *kolkhozniks* themselves were spontaneously carrying out mergers. Khrushchev remained the leading spokesman for this new idea and developed it subsequently. In a *Pravda* article of April 25, 1950, he held out the prospect that, having merged, *kolkhozes* would be able 'to build fine, well-constructed villages into which the *kolkhozniks* would be moved from the small, badly built villages. In these new villages good cultural and living conditions will be created.' At the same time, the reform was clearly intended to facilitate party control over the farms. Fewer units would require fewer politically reliable chairmen, for example, and Khrushchev stressed 'the enormous importance in the merging of *kolkhozes* of the selection and promotion of leading *kolkhoz* cadres and of work with *kolkhoz* chairmen'.[150]

The utopian aspect of the campaign culminated in the publication in *Pravda* on March 4, 1951, of a speech in which Khrushchev envisaged the *kolkhoznik* building himself a four-roomed house—'one room can no longer satisfy him'—in large modern 'agrotowns' (or '*kolkhoz* settlements', as he said he preferred to call them) with proper drains, electricity, street-lighting and pavements. Khrushchev proposed that in these urban-type settlements the peasants should retain only a small portion of their plots outside their homes, and that the rest should be in a common allotment area outside the village.

The day after the publication of this article, *Pravda* announced that a mistake had been made: it should have been accompanied by a note saying it was 'for discussion purposes' only.[151] This disavowal of the article's official status signified disapproval by Stalin, and was followed by criticism of the 'agrotown' idea by Beria's supporters ('Fantastic plans for

[44]

peasant resettlement'[152]) and, more notably, by Malenkov at the 19th party congress in October, 1952. He denounced it for reflecting 'a wrong, consumer approach to questions of collective farm development'—i.e. for overstressing the peasants' welfare. 'The mistake', according to Malenkov, 'was to forget the major production tasks of the collective farms and give prominence to tasks that derive from them, to consumer tasks connected with welfare amenities in the collective farms. These tasks . . . are not major tasks and they can be carried out successfully only if collective farm production is further developed.'[153] Nothing more was heard of the 'agrotown' scheme[154] and Khrushchev's responsibility for agriculture was diminished. But the campaign for *kolkhoz* merging proceeded. During 1950, the number of *kolkhozes* was reduced, because of merging, from 252,000 to 123,000[155]; by October, 1952, it was down to 97,000.[156]

The third issue in dispute concerned the MTS and the proposal to sell their machinery to the *kolkhozes*. The only overt sign of this dispute was Stalin's rebuttal of the proposal in a letter to two economists who had advocated it, Sanina and Venzher, in *Pravda* of October 4, 1952. According to Stalin, Sanina and Venzher had recalled the original intention of making the MTS *kolkhoz* property (see p. 39) and had argued that this was not done in the early days of collectivisation because the *kolkhozes* could not afford to buy the machinery, but that now they were rich enough to do so. Stalin rejected the proposal on the ground that only the State had the resources to invest in agricultural machinery and replace it when obsolete; that the *kolkhozes* should not own their basic means of production, and that agricultural machinery should not be marketed.

STALIN'S LEGACY

The main features of Stalin's peasant policy were thus:

(a) A ruthless and total disregard of peasant interests. Collectivisation under him was a form of subjugation and exploitation more severe and complete than the serfdom abolished in 1861.

(b) Little encouragement for the collectivised peasants to produce except on their own private plots, and less concern for methods of production than for methods of procuring production for the State.

[45]

(c)   The depression of peasant living standards,[157] and a low level of investment in agriculture as a whole.

Criticism of this policy during the Khrushchev era went a long way towards admitting the damage it had done:

'The sorry state of agriculture [in the immediate post-war years] was also the result of deficiencies in the control of agriculture during the cult of Stalin's personality. Excessive centralisation of the planning and control of agricultural production stifled the initiative of the *kolkhozes*; the high rate of taxation and low procurement prices, which frequently did not even cover production costs, limited the possibilities of expanding production and undermined the *kolkhozniks'* material incentives. A serious brake on the development of agriculture in these and subsequent years were the harmful and baseless theories and dogmas [i.e. Lysenkoism] (*see* p. 77) propagated in the biological and agronomical sciences.[158]'

And:

'The ignoring of the Leninist principle of material incentives for agricultural workers sprang from Stalin's underestimation of the rôle of the peasantry as an ally of the working class ... Stalin's opinions about peasants were biased and often malevolent. He liked to repeat the well-known words of V. I. Lenin that the peasantry "engenders capitalism and bourgeoisie constantly, daily, hourly, spontaneously, and on a mass scale" ... In many of Stalin's utterances, and especially in his practical direction of agriculture, there was often revealed a presumptuous, arrogant attitude towards the *"muzhik"*, mistrust and suspicion towards agricultural workers.''[159]

Khrushchev, in his 'secret' speech, told the 20th party congress that the last time Stalin visited a village was in January, 1928, and that 'he never even noticed the difficult situation in agriculture.'[160]

SOURCES

1. Marx and Engels, Vol. 1, pp. 32–61.
2. *Ibid.*, Vol. 2, pp. 393–4.
3. *Ibid.*, p. 397.
4. RSFSR *Laws*, 1917, 1:3 (IKP, Vol. 1, p. 17).
5. RSFSR *Laws,* 1918, 25:346 (IKP, Vol. 1, p. 19).
6. Lenin, Vol. 28, p. 156.

7. Lenin told the Tenth Party Congress: 'We must say straight out that the peasantry is dissatisfied with the kind of relationship which has grown up between us, and that they do not wish it and will not carry on existing like this. There is no

question about it. Their will has been clearly expressed ... We are sufficiently sober politicians to say straight out: let us change our policy towards the peasants. We can no longer maintain the situation which has existed so far' (Vol. 32, pp. 192–3). The Antonov peasant rising was not suppressed until the summer of 1924 (Popov, Part 2, p. 158), and some of its leaders survived to fight again, against collectivisation in 1930 (Sharova, p. 155). Further details about the rising are in BSE, first edition, vol. 3, p. 98.

8. RSFSR *Laws*, 1922, 36: 426; USSR *Laws*, 1925, 26:183.

9. Lenin, Vol. 33, pp. 386–7.

10. *Pravda*, April 24, 1925.

11. *Pravda*, November 13–15, 1925.

12. Stalin, Vol. 11, p. 86. The statistical basis for this statement is doubtful, and considered at length in *Soviet Studies*, April, 1967, by J. F. Karcz.

13. Stalin, Vol. 11, pp. 83, 96.

14. *Ibid.*, pp. 159–60.

15. *Ibid.*, pp. 318–19. This speech to the Politburo in February, 1929, was first published in 1949.

16. *Sotsialistichesky Vestnik*, 1929, No. 9.

17. *Pravda*, November 26, 1929.

18. Stalin, Vol. 11, p. 206.

19. Stalin, Vol. 12, p. 166.

20. KS Kh, p. 258.

21. This decree, one of the most important in the collectivi-

sation campaign, is omitted from the published collections of documents on the period. It is summarised, however, in Danilov, pp. 39, 104, and in *Voprosi Istorii*, 1963, No. 5 (Bogdenko, p. 31). See also Fainsod, p. 242.

22. Fainsod, p. 242.

23. *Voprosi Istorii*, 1963, No. 5, p. 31.

24. *Ibid.*

25. Fainsod, p. 243.

26. Danilov, p. 105.

27. *Voprosi Istorii*, 1963, No. 5, p. 32.

28. KS Kh, p. 267. According to Danilov (p. 38) already by the summer of 1930 over 400 million roubles of *kulak* property has been confiscated, amounting to 23 per cent of *kolkhoz* property.

29. *Voprosi Istorii*, 1963, No. 5, p. 32.

30. Fainsod, p. 242. In 1934, the OGPU were supposed to select deported *kulaks* for rehabilitation if they had worked hard and shown loyalty to the régime (KS Kh, p. 505).

31. KS Kh, p. 254.

32. Sharova, pp. 148–51.

33. These attempts have been led by S. P. Trapeznikov, head of the party Central Committee's department for science and educational institutions, who under Khrushchev was attacked by other historians for the crudity of his efforts at whitewashing collectivisation (Sharova, pp. 157–8). Trapeznikov condemned 'incorrect assessments of

collectivisation' and 'over-emphasis on certain episodes', in *Pravda* of October 8, 1965. Further condemnation of 'the negative portrayal of collectivisation', and of those who 'question the necessity of liquidating the *kulaks* as a class', appeared in *Selskaya Zhizn* of December 29, 1965, and February 25, 1966. *Kommunist*, 1967, No. 11, singled out for special denunciation Danilov's 'Outline History of the collectivisation of agriculture in the Union Republics', and his article on collectivisation in the *Soviet Historical Encyclopaedia*, which are probably the frankest accounts by a Soviet historian.

34. Jasny, p. 324, has shown on the basis of official data that well over half the horses and cattle outside State farms, and about two-thirds of the pigs, sheep and goats, disappeared during 1928–33 as a result of collectivisation.

35. Danilov, p. 45.

36. *Ibid.*, Stalin said in November, 1928, that *kulaks* constituted only five per cent of the peasantry (Stalin, vol. 11, p. 265). The estimate for the Ukraine in 1927 was only four per cent, according to Danilov (p. 171).

37. *Ibid.*, p. 446.

38. *Ibid.*, p. 45.

39. *Ibid.*, pp. 38, 104.

40. *Ibid.*, pp. 89, 104.

41. Sharova, p. 155.

42. Danilov, pp. 235–6.

43. *Ibid.*, p. 281.

44. *Ibid.*, p. 408.

45. *Ibid.*, pp. 480–1. According to a subsequent Soviet legend, 'the well-known English spy', Lawrence of Arabia, directed resistance to collectivisation in Turkmenistan (*Kommunist*, May 25, 1968).

46. The progress of collectivisation, in terms of peasant families collectivised, was as follows, according to Prokopovicz, citing official sources: October, 1929—4·1 per cent; January 20, 1930—21 per cent; March 10, 1930—58 per cent. In the period October–December, 1929, 2·4 million peasant families were collectivised at an average daily rate of 30,000 families, according to Danilov (p. 40).

47. Danilov (p. 46) comments: 'In this article, Stalin shifted all the responsibility for the mistakes on to local officials and sweepingly accused them of bungling. The contents and tone of the article were unexpected for the party and caused some disarray among party cadres'.

48. Thus, in March, 1937, he told the party Central Committee: 'You may remember 1930, when our party comrades thought they could solve the most complex question of shifting the peasantry towards collectivisation in some three or four months, and when the party Central Committee found itself compelled to restrain the over-zealous

comrades. It was one of the most dangerous periods in the life of our party' (Stalin, Vol. 14, p. 235).

49. KS Kh, p. 287.
50. The percentage was 21·4 in August, 1930, according to SIE, Vol. 7, p. 491.
51. Danilov, p. 47.
52. SIE, Vol. 7, p. 492.
53. KS Kh, pp. 423–4.
54. *Ibid.*, pp. 448, 451.
55. *Sotsialisticheskaya Zakonnost*, 1936, No. 8, p. 5.
56. Stalin, Vol. 13, p. 209.
57. *Ibid.*, p. 392.
58. *Vyshinsky*, pp. 99–103.
59. *Pravda*, August 23, 1932.
60. Stalin, Vol. 13, p. 204.
61. Golyakov, p. 271.
62. ESP, p. 309.
63. Stalin, Vol. 13, p. 228; Danilov, p. 57.
64. KS Kh, p. 432.
65. Danilov, p. 136.
66. The Central Committee resolution of January 11, 1933, accused them of 'falling under the influence of these wrecking elements', and said, 'some party members who penetrated the party for careerist reasons are allying themselves with the enemies of the *kolkhozes*'.
67. Fainsod, pp. 286–7, 289.
68. *Izvestiya*, March 12, 1933.
69. Fainsod, p. 185.
70. Danilov, p. 58.
71. *Istoriya Kommunisticheskoi Partii Sovetskogo Soyuza*, p. 463. A *kulak* household (which sometimes extended beyond one family) seems to have averaged five to six persons. This means that up to 1·4 million per-

sons are officially admitted to have been deported. Stalin told Churchill that 10 million *kulaks* had to be dealt with, and that 'the great bulk' were 'wiped out', others being deported to Siberia. (W. S. Churchill, *The Second World War*, Vol. IV, pp. 447–8).
72. *Planovoe Khozyaistvo*, 1929, No. 8, p. 49 (Strumilin).
73. *Voprosi Istorii*, 1962, No. 4, p. 68.
74. Stalin, Vol. 11, p. 265.
75. A detailed discussion, including mortality estimates, is in *Soviet Studies*, January, 1964, pp. 250–284 (Dalrymple). See also Prokopovicz, p. 66.
76. Grain exports were as follows (in million centners): 1929—2·6; 1930—48·4; 1931—51·8 (SIE, Vol. 7, p. 493).
77. Khrushchev's speech in *Pravda*, March 10, 1963.
78. *Soviet Studies*, January, 1964, pp. 261–2.
79. 'People are not angels', by I. F. Stadnyuk, published in *Neva*, December, 1962, and in an English translation by Mono Press, London, 1963. The following passage appears on p. 119 of the translation:

'Hunger: a terrible, soul-chilling word of darkness. Those who have never experienced it cannot imagine what suffering hunger causes. There is nothing worse for the man—the head of the family—than the sense of his own helplessness in face of his wife's prayers, when she cannot find food for her hungry children. There is nothing more terrible for the mother than the sight of her emaciated enfeebled children who through hunger have forgotten to smile.

'If it were only for a week or a month, but it is for many months that most of the local families have nothing to put on the table. All the cellars were swept clean, not a single hen remained in the village: even the beetroot seeds have been consumed. Everyone was waiting for the spring as they have never waited for anything. They were waiting for the time when the earth in the gardens was unfrozen so that they could dig up the plots where potatoes had grown last year in the hope of finding some left behind. They were waiting for the live bark and swelling buds on the lime-trees. And later on there would be nettles and goosefoot and sorrel. They were hoping that nature would give at least some help to man.

'But the spring suddenly withdrew.

'The first who died from hunger were the men. Later on the children. And last of all, the women. But before they died, people often lost their senses and ceased to be human beings.'

80. Danilov, pp. 293–4.
81. Jasny, p. 323.

82. Danilov, pp. 285–92.
83. Ibid., p. 252.
84. Ibid., pp. 491–2.
85. Prokopovicz, p. 169.
86. Danilov, p. 58.
87. The first model statutes were issued in March, 1930, but did not provide an effective legal framework during the collectivisation period (KS Kh, pp. 282–7, 531–9).
88. BSE, second edition, Vol. 16, p. 298.
89. KS Kh, p. 441.
90. The kolkhoz markets had been established by a decree of May 6, 1932 (KS Kh, p. 411), which gave legal sanction to the existing practice under which peasants sold food at exorbitant prices to city dwellers. Making a virtue of necessity, the decree declared: 'The Soviet régime has found it possible, as a means of supplying the urban population, to practise, together with the method of State grain deliveries, another method, the method of trading in grain by the kolkhozes and kolkhozniks themselves'. But those who brought their grain to market before fulfilling their State deliveries and replenishing their seed reserves were threatened with up to ten years in a concentration camp under the decree 'on speculation' of August 22, 1932 (decree of December 2, 1932, KS Kh, p. 427). Official estimates showed that almost a quarter of the total food

turnover in 1938 was accounted for by these markets (Jasny, p. 385).

91. BSE, second edition, Vol. 16, p. 300.
92. KS Kh, pp. 544–54.
93. SIE, Vol. 7, p. 494. 'The prices for grain and many other products were symbolic (ten to 12 times lower than market prices). This system undermined the *kolkhozniks'* incentive to develop socialised production.'
94. Volin, p. 68.
95. KS Kh, p. 453.
96. *Ibid.*, p. 464.
97. Jasny, pp. 373–4; *Spravochnik*, p. 248; IKP, Vol. 2, pp. 136–9.
98. Jasny, p. 370.
99. *Ibid.*
100. Volin, p. 37; Jasny, p. 738.
101. By a decree of April 8, 1940, which said that the old system of basing deliveries on planned sown area had led 'to attempts by *kolkhozes* to achieve reduced plans for sowing grain . . . [and] to a reduction of sown areas' (IKP, Vol. 2, p. 135).
102. Korovyakovsky, pp. 32–3.
103. Stalin, Vol. 14, pp. 53–4.
104. Prokopovicz, p. 205.
105. Jasny, p. 346.
106. *Planovoe Khozyaistvo*, 1939, No. 7.
107. *Jasny*, p. 699.
108. *XVIII S'ezd VKP (b)*, p. 119.
109. *Ibid.*
110. KPSS, Vol. 2, p. 939.
111. IKP, Vol. 2, p. 111.
112. *Ibid.*

113. Decree of Sixth Congress of Soviets of March 17, 1931 (KS Kh, p. 375).
114. *Ibid.*
115. Danilov, p. 144; Jasny, p. 403; Gsovski, Vol. 1, p. 741.
116. Gsovski, Vol. 1, p. 743.
117. Jasny, pp. 690–2.
118. IKP, Vol. 2, p. 42.
119. Gsovski, Vol. 2, p. 738.
120. KS Kh, p. 409.
121. *XVIII S'ezd VKP (b)*, pp. 117–18.
122. KS Kh, p. 179.
123. *Ibid.*, p. 445.
124. SIE, Vol. 9, p. 207.
125. *Ibid.*, p. 206.
126. KS Kh, p. 488.
127. *Ibid.*, p. 468 (decree of September 2, 1933).
128. *Ibid.*, pp. 555–60 (Statutes of the MTS Tractor Driver, approved on September 21, 1933).
129. *Ibid.*, p. 471 (decree of September 21, 1933).
130. *XVIII S'ezd VKP (b)*, pp. 109–10.
131. *Sovetskoe Gosudarstvo i Pravo*, 1965, No. 3, p. 24; Conquest, p. 128.
132. Voznesensky, pp. 157–60.
133. The proportion of women tractor-drivers rose from four per cent in 1940 to 45 per cent in 1942, and of women combine operators from six per cent to 43 per cent (Voznesensky, pp. 92–93).
134. IKP, Vol. 2, p. 219.
135. *See* p. 35 (para. (d)).
136. Volin, p. 20.
137. KPSS, Vol. 2, p. 1038.
138. *Pravda*, September 19, 1947.
139. IKP, Vol. 2, p. 322.

140. *Ibid.*

141. By a Central Committee Plenum of November, 1934 (KS Kh, p. 516), which abolished the MTS 'Political Departments' set up in January, 1933.

142. KPSS, Vol. 2, p. 1092.

143. IKP, Vol. 2, p. 309.

144. Danilov, pp. 532–3.

145. *Ibid.*, p. 536.

146. KPSS, Vol. 2, p. 1046.

147. For details *see* Volin, pp. 181–3.

148. *Pravda*, December 10, 1963.

149. Conquest, pp. 112–28.

150. *Pravda*, June 28, 1950.

151. *Pravda*, March 5, 1951; Ilichev described to the 22nd Party Congress how the article aroused Stalin's anger and the 'correction' was inserted on his orders.

152. *Kommunist* (Armenia), March 20, 1951 (Arutinov); *Bakinsky Rabochy*, May 25, 1951 (Bagirov).

153. *Pravda*, October 6, 1952, p. 5.

154. There were occasional references to 'agrotowns' under Khrushchev's régime, but he never reverted to the scheme as such.

155. *Sotsialisticheskoe Zemledelie*, March 3, 1951.

156. *Pravda*, October 6, 1952, p. 5.

157. The average income of *kolkhozniks* in 1938 was 20 per cent or more below that of the peasants before collectivisation, according to Jasny, p. 702.

158. SIE, Vol. 7, pp. 497–8.

159. *Kommunist*, 1963, No. 6, p. 26.

160. The Dethronement of Stalin, pp. 29–30.

II

The Khrushchev Period

The derelict state of agriculture presented Stalin's successor's with their biggest problem, for it imperilled the whole national economy. It is significant that every defeated leader in the post-Stalin power struggle (including Khrushchev after his 'resignation' in October, 1964) was saddled immediately after his downfall with responsibility for agricultural failures.

Thus: 'For the purposes of undermining the collective farm system and causing food difficulties in our country, Beria sabotaged in every kind of way, and impeded the implementation of the most important party and government measures directed towards an upsurge of the economy of the collective and State farms[1]...'

Malenkov's resignation statement, read to the Supreme Soviet on February 8, 1955, declared: 'I see particularly clearly my fault and responsibility for the unsatisfactory state of affairs in agriculture[2]...'

The 'anti-party group' (Molotov, Malenkov, Kaganovich and others defeated in June, 1957) were found to be: 'zealous opponents of the party's measures in agriculture. Responsible for failures in this field in the past, they would not admit our present successes. These successes were achieved despite them, against them, in conflict with them.'[3]

At the March, 1965, Central Committee plenum, the Kazakh First Secretary claimed that 'we would have ruined agriculture in Kazakhstan' if Khrushchev's instructions had been strictly followed, and added: 'You all know how things used to be done. People would arrive, give instructions and order everybody about. We are talking gently about it at the moment, but you all know this was Comrade Khrushchev's work.'[4]

THE 1953 REFORMS

The first measures of the post-Stalin régime (after Beria's arrest) were a hurried attempt to revive agriculture by offering conces-

[53]

sions to the peasants. Most of these were announced by Malenkov to the Supreme Soviet in August, 1953, and by Khrushchev at a Central Committee plenum the following month. For the first time since collectivisation, the agricultural situation was treated with a measure of frankness: certain failings and the need for changes were admitted. The major admission was that agricultural production, especially livestock farming, 'does not fully satisfy the growing requirements of the population for food', chiefly because of 'the violation in agriculture of the principle of material incentives'.[5]

The concessions, designed to encourage production by raising incentives, were largely financial. They included tax concessions (a halving of the tax burden on *kolkhoz* households and cancellation of arrears)[6] and price increases for agricultural produce. The price for above-quota grain deliveries was raised nine times,[7] and increased considerably for compulsory and above-quota deliveries of other produce—the most substantial rise being by five and a half times for compulsory meat deliveries.[8] Compulsory delivery quotas for animal products, potatoes and vegetables were cut and there was also the cautious promise of a more relaxed attitude towards the private plot, especially towards private livestock farming. Malenkov went furthest when he declared: 'The government and party Central Committee have also decided seriously to correct and alter the incorrect attitude which has become established among us towards the personal plots of the *kolkhozniks*.'[9] This relatively friendly gesture towards the private sector was, however, accompanied by a measure intended to ensure that it did not expand at the expense of the communal sector. Article 6 of the new tax law provided that any household in which a member failed to fulfil his minimum annual labour-days would have its tax increased by 50 per cent.[10] The wartime minimum was retained after the war, and was further raised in 1954.[11]

The concessions were accompanied by a strengthening of administrative, and especially party, controls. Khrushchev remarked: 'The necessity for bringing party leaders closer to the decisive sectors of production has become urgent.'[12] The post of MTS Deputy Director for Political Affairs was abolished, and party control over the *kolkhoz* was vested instead in the local *raion* party committee, the Secretary of which was responsible through 'instructors' attached to each farm for all party work. Meanwhile, the MTS were strengthened by a provision that tractor drivers should henceforth be full-time MTS employees with higher wages and better training facilities.[13]

Although the 1953 reforms, especially the financial concessions, were beneficial, they made little impact on the basic problem of inadequate incentives. Agricultural prices, even after the increases, were still well below production costs, and the terms of trade—the relationship between prices of agricultural products and of manufactured consumer-goods—remained unfavourable for the peasantry. Agricultural prices fixed by the State had remained basically unchanged since the beginning of collectivisation,[14] while retail prices of manufactured consumer goods had risen almost tenfold between 1932 and 1952.[15] As a result of the 1953 and subsequent price increases, average prices for all agricultural products (for compulsory and above-quota purchases) almost trebled between 1952 and 1957,[16] but still failed to stimulate production.

1954–1958

From the end of 1953, Khrushchev dominated the political scene (he became First Secretary in September) and made agriculture his special concern. He devoted more time and energy to agricultural affairs than to any other, and constantly toured the countryside giving detailed instructions and promoting his favourite schemes. The Khrushchev era in Soviet agriculture falls roughly into two periods: from 1954 until 1958, when even according to his subsequent critics his policies largely paid off and the condition of the peasantry noticeably improved; and from 1958 until 1964, years characterised by stagnation.

(a) THE VIRGIN LANDS PROJECT

The first of Khrushchev's major schemes was the Virgin Lands project, which he launched in a speech of February 23, 1954.[17] Under this, by the end of 1961, about 100 million acres, mostly in Kazakhstan and southern Siberia, were brought under cultivation—an area equal to that under plough in Canada, and which increased the total sown area in the Soviet Union by a little over a quarter.[18] The labour force for this huge task was provided mostly by

[55]

'volunteers' mobilised from all over the country. State farms, not *Kolkhozes*, were the favoured organisation for the new territories. The scheme meant that for several successive years the established farming areas of the Soviet Union suffered more than usually from a shortage of machinery, technical supplies and specialists, as these resources had to be diverted to the new territories.[19] The non-black-earth districts of central and northern Russia seem to have suffered most from neglect as a result of this diversion of men and materials.[20]

The Virgin Lands project helped the régime to cope with its immediate difficulties over grain, but offered no long-term solution to them. The post-Khrushchev régime, while not denouncing the scheme as a whole, has severely criticised it for being carried out over-hastily, thus causing erosion ('several million hectares of newly ploughed land fell out of use, and it is now necessary to carry out urgent measures to convert them to pasture by sowing perennial grasses')[21] and soil exhaustion through continuous cropping ('the rapid exhaustion of the soil's fertility and the heavy infestation of the fields with weeds'[22]).

(b) MAIZE

A year later[23] Khrushchev launched another idea intended as a further solution to the grain problem: a large-scale restructuring of the crop-pattern based on an expansion of the area sown to maize. He called for the maize area to be increased almost seven times, from 3½ million hectares in 1953 to 28 million hectares by 1960. He claimed that maize could be used as cattle-fodder even if it did not ripen, and could therefore be sown almost anywhere.

The result of this campaign was a vast over-extension of the maize area and its cultivation in totally unsuitable districts. By the end of the Khrushchev period, the maize area had in fact grown tenfold.[24] Not only did this involve a lot of wasted effort, but it hampered the cultivation of other crops, for which peak seasonal needs for labour and machinery overlapped those for maize.

(c) COLLECTIVE FARM REFORMS

Khrushchev was less bold in his first reforms of the collective farm system. The problem was to encourage local initiative and flexibility while at the same time strengthening party controls. The basic incompatibility of these two objectives left little scope for radical innovation.

The first reform, a decree of March 9, 1955,[25] ostensibly granted the *kolkhozes* greater powers to decide their own crop-patterns and livestock holdings. It provided that the farms should have planned for them only their delivery quotas and procurement targets, and not their crop areas or the type and quantity of their animal holdings. 'The new system of planning', it stated, 'will give the collective farms greater opportunities for showing administrative initiative in utilising reserves of collective farm production.' But there was a safeguard: 'Where the plan presented by the collective farm does not ensure fulfilment by it of obligatory deliveries and the payment in kind for MTS work...the *raion* executive committee is to recommend the collective farm to introduce the necessary alterations.'

Another safeguard was the despatch, between April and July, 1955, of 30,000 party-selected organisers from the towns as chairmen of the collective farms. This meant that about a third of the farms had new, politically vetted leaders. But most of these had no direct experience of agriculture so that they had to undergo courses to 'acquaint themselves with the economics and organisation of production'.[26]

Despite considerable propaganda about its liberating effect, the 'new planning system' made little difference to traditional ways of imposing detailed agricultural tasks on the farms. The reality behind the pretence was described at the March, 1965, plenum:

'The imposition of the crop-pattern caused great harm, and moreover, it was given almost overriding importance in the improvement of agriculture. We *obkom* secretaries all remember how we were summoned every year to the Agricultural Department for the RSFSR of the CPSU Central Committee, where the structure of sown areas was fixed, our signatures under this structure were collected under pressure, and then the whole thing was presented as a proposal from below.'[27]

Apart from anything else, Khrushchev's maize programme was clearly incompatible with any genuine freedom of choice in cropping patterns. The farms' compulsory delivery targets, in any case, largely determined what crops they grew, and what livestock they kept.

Another much-publicised reform which created an illusion of liberalisation was a decree of March 6, 1956, 'on the agricultural artel statutes and the further development of the *kolkhozniks'* initiative in organising *kolkhoz* production and administering the affairs of the artel'.[28] Ostensibly, its purpose was to develop local initiative by enabling farms to amend their own statutes: *'Kolkhozes* themselves can decide questions of *kolkhoz* life even more independently than hitherto . . . it is necessary to recommend and advise *kolkhozes* . . . to supplement and amend certain articles of their statutes, taking the local concrete conditions of the *kolkhoz* into account.' But the only important amendments envisaged were that the *kolkhozes* should set their own minima for labour-days to be worked on the farm (they had already been entitled to do this in 1954[29]), and fix the size of private plots and the number of private cattle.

The private sector, the decree made clear, must be reduced, not expanded. The size of plots should be decided on the basis of the effort put into the communal economy by individual *kolkhozniks*, and in some cases the plots should be withdrawn altogether. As for private livestock, 'in many regions . . . it is hardly necessary to keep the previously established number of animals'. The decree also recommended the introduction of monthly advances in money and periodic advances in kind to *kolkhozniks*.[30] (Provision for this had been made in the 1935 statutes, but most farms did not have enough income.)

A feature of the 1954–8 period was the start of a trend towards reducing the number of *kolkhozes*, both by merging them into larger units and by converting weak or run-down ones into *sovkhozes*. As a result of mergers and conversions the number of *kolkhozes* fell from 91,200 in 1953 to 67,700 in 1958. The trend continued and by the end of 1964 there were only 37,000. Some, it was stated after Khrushchev's fall, were so large as to be 'completely unmanageable'.[31]

(d) ABOLITION OF THE MTS

The most far-reaching reform of this period was the abolition of the MTS and the associated simplification of the agricultural deliveries and price system, in 1958.

The possibility of transferring MTS machinery to the *kolkhozes* had been mooted in Stalin's time, but he had stamped on the idea (see Section I, p. 45). Khrushchev revived it in a speech on January 22, 1958,[32] arguing that while it had been impracticable earlier, it was now feasible because of the *kolkhozes'* greater financial and organisational strength. It would, he stressed, overcome the difficulties arising from the fact that 'there are two bosses for one piece of land—the *kolkhoz* and the MTS'. The latter, he proposed, should be converted into repair stations (RTS), which would also be responsible for the sale to the farms of machinery, spares, fuel and other technical supplies.

Perhaps the most important consideration was that 'the MTS have ceased to play the political rôle they played during the first stage of *kolkhoz* construction', and that the *kolkhoz* party organisations were sufficiently strong to ensure political control together with the local *raion* party committees which in September, 1953, had taken over the functions of the MTS Political Affairs Department (see p. 42). Khrushchev later revealed[33] that in 1958, 'nearly all farms had party organisations, with an average membership of 20' (whereas at the September, 1953, plenum, 20 per cent of the farms had no such bodies). Khrushchev's proposals were embodied in 'Theses',[34] supposedly for public discussion and, unaltered in any essential, in a decree of March 31, 1958.[35]

By July 1, 1959, 94 per cent of the *kolkhozes* had bought MTS machinery for cash or on credit, including 512,000 tractors and 221,000 combines. They had also bought 100,000 new tractors and 25,000 combines.[36] During 1958–9 they spent a total of 32 milliard (old) roubles on machinery, of which 18 milliard was for the MTS machinery.[37] The reform involved the transfer to the *kolkhozes* of not only MTS machinery, but also most of its personnel. According to Khrushchev there were 1.5 million machine operators and 186,000 officials and engineering-technical personnel.[38] Their transfer meant a big expansion of the *kolkhoz* 'aristocracy' of better-paid specialists (the machine operators retained their privilege of guaranteed minimum pay),[39] and taking them on their payroll added to the financial difficulties of *kolkhozes* with insufficient funds to pay for MTS machinery.

The abolition of the MTS had two serious disadvantages, it was admitted after Khrushchev's departure. Firstly, financially weak *kolkhozes* were constrained to repay in one year credits used to acquire machinery, although this was beyond their means and they became deeply indebted.[40] In 1965, 'several thousand' *kolkhozes* were still unable to acquire their own machinery.[41] Secondly, the reform caused the disintegration of the repair service for agricultural machinery as the RTS failed to fulfil the functions formerly performed by the MTS.[42]

(e) REFORM OF AGRICULTURAL DELIVERIES AND PRICE SYSTEM

The abolition of the MTS, one of the functions of which had been to act as a procurement agency for agricultural products, necessitated a reform of the procurement mechanism. Moreover, since 1953 there had been a tendency for the distinction between obligatory and above-quota deliveries, especially the price differential between them, to diminish. Obligatory deliveries from private plots had been abolished, first for grain in 1954,[43] and then for other products in 1957.[44] Steps were taken under a decree of June 18, 1958,[45] to unify and simplify the procurement procedure by doing away with the 'obligatory' and 'above-quota' system, and substituting a single sytem of planned State procurements at unified prices. The new system of planned procurements was, however, no less obligatory for the *kolkhozes* than the old.

The decree said that the procurement plan should be fixed 'for republics, *krais*, *oblasts*, State and collective farms for several years. But annual procurement plans may be corrected to allow for increases according to the conditions of the year and the harvest of individual crops'. Plans were to be based on the same 'per hectare principle'[46] hitherto applied for calculating obligatory deliveries and, according to Khrushchev,[47] were to 'proceed from the level of deliveries achieved' under the old system, but 'taking into account the increased requirements of the State'.

On the new unified prices, the decree said they should 'take into account the need to cover *kolkhoz* costs . . . and to create the necessary [capital] accumulation'. The State's total bill for procurements, Khrushchev made clear, should not exceed that under the old arrangements.[48] Prices should be both stable and flexible, i.e., like the procurement plans, they should remain basically unchanged over a longish period, varying only in abnormally good or bad years. They should also, more than hitherto, 'be differentiated according to the different zones of the country, taking natural, climatic and economic differences into account'.[49] All indebtedness in respect of compulsory deliveries and payments in kind was written off.

The new system seemed to promise a more stable and equitable procedure for extracting produce from the farms, but in practice it brought little improvement, for two main reasons: the procurement plans were fixed far too high and were always being altered; and the unified prices were far too low and failed to cover costs, let alone capital accumulation. Brezhnev admitted in 1965 that 'procurement prices for many agricultural products do not cover their production costs. As a result State and collective farms are suffering great losses... The present procurements system brings uncertainty into [the farms'] work and does not allow them to plan their production correctly. Procurement plans ... are often received with great delay, and only for one year. In addition, these plans are frequently altered while procurements are in progress, and collective and State farms are given additional tasks often exceeding what had been planned for them.'[50]

He disclosed that grain procurements had been forced so high that the farms had been unable to replenish their seed stocks and had had to buy back from the State millions of tons of seed.[51] According to Mazurov (then Party First Secretary of Belorussia and now a member of the Politburo), planned meat procurements were so high that *kolkhozes* had to slaughter their animals prematurely to fulfil them.[52] The official statistical journal revealed that 'in many regions' *kolkhozes* were making a loss of 25 per cent on cattle sales and 22 per cent on milk sales.[53]

1959–1964

The stagnation of agriculture after 1958 was highlighted at the January, 1961, Central Committee plenum, at which Khrushchev confessed that production was still not enough to meet the people's needs, and angrily blamed this on bureaucratic and corrupt officials.

'These people [officials submitting false returns] should be turned out of the party. They are not Communists, but hangers-on. These people should be brought to trial ... and punished regardless of personalities. If we do not put matters right, plans will be fulfilled only on paper while in fact there is a shortfall in production. You

[61]

can't make pancakes out of statistics . . . Only enemies of the Socialist State can behave in such a way. Without caring about the state
of affairs in the *raions*, in the *kolkhozes*, or in the *oblasts* such
people look at everything only from their own position . . .'⁵⁴

The plenum also revealed some of the grotesque inefficiencies
and anomalies which had grown up. These were exemplified
by the case of the *obkom* Secretary in Kirgizia who 'forced
those in charge of *raions* and *kolkhozes* to buy butter in the
shops and deliver it in fulfilment of their milk delivery plan'.⁵⁵

Khrushchev's handling of agriculture after 1958 was characterised by his increasingly impatient search for an administrative solution to its problems, and the launching of unrealistic
crash programmes such as that for a vast expansion of chemi-
cal fertiliser production, or for the ploughing up of huge areas
of meadow and grassland. The period was marked by administrative reorganisation and shake-ups, and the constant chiv-
vying, public bullying and replacement of officials—there were
three changes of Minister of Agriculture in little over two
years.⁵⁶ This stirred things up superficially, but left the funda-
mentals unchanged.

(*a*) REFORM OF MINISTRY OF AGRICULTURE
AND
ESTABLISHMENT OF PROCUREMENTS COMMITTEE

Khrushchev's proposal at the January, 1961, plenum that the
Ministry of Agriculture should be stripped of its policy-making
and executive functions and concern itself mainly with the
propagation of modern scientific methods was embodied in a
decree of February 20, 1961.⁵⁷ This left the Ministry responsible for such matters as seed selection, experimental stations,
scientific institutes, and crop diseases and pests. Some of its
former functions passed to the State Planning Commission,
Gosplan, and the Central Statistical Office. The reform was
presented as a victory over bureaucracy, and this was subsequently symbolised in the removal of the Ministry's offices to
the country outside Moscow. At the same time, however (by
another decree published the same day⁵⁸), a new central organ
with local subsidiaries was established to replace the RTS:
Soyuzselkhoztekhnika (The All-Union Association of the USSR
Council of Ministers for the sale of agricultural equipment,
spares, mineral fertiliser and other technical equipment, and

the organisation of the repair and utilisation of machinery on collective and State farms).

Another of Khrushchev's proposals at the January, 1961, plenum was to establish a State Committee for Procurements in charge of a reorganised procurements system. This idea was to link the procurement agency more closely to the farms so that it could eliminate the various forms of defrauding which had grown up and influence the farms in production as well as supervise their deliveries. ('The purchaser must also be the organiser of production ... Through the procurement system, the state of affairs on State and collective farms can be studied.'[59]) He suggested that the farms and the local procurement agency should conclude 'contracts' detailing the produce to be delivered and the delivery dates. This system was introduced by two decrees of February 25, 1961.[60] The 'contracts' were to be concluded for periods of two to five years, and establish annual obligations for each farm in accordance with targets already planned for each region. Neither party to the 'contract' was therefore a free agent, nor was there any question of free bargaining. The reality remained a bureaucratically enforced, compulsory delivery system. Moreover, a new army of inspectors was created to supervise it. One inspector for every three to seven farms was responsible for 'the organisation of purchases and control over fulfilment of State plans for purchases ... studying the situation and the prospects for the further development of agricultural production ... the conclusion of contracts ... control over the fulfilment of contracts ... [and] participation in working out measures for the further development of production ...'[61]

(b) FURTHER ADMINISTRATIVE REFORMS

A year later, at the March, 1962, plenum, Khrushchev introduced another and more sweeping reform of the administration of agriculture.

He admitted that 'the party and all the Soviet people are seriously disturbed at the state of agriculture', that the Seven-Year Plan for agriculture was 'seriously endangered', and that unless production was increased considerably in the next few years, 'we will place the country in great difficulties and the cause of building Communism will suffer a heavy blow'.[62]

His remedy was to subject the farms to a tighter and more detailed form of supervision than ever.

'We have more than enough departments which carry out the general management of agriculture. But what we do not have is a department which would manage agriculture, deal with the organisation of production and procurement, go deeply into the needs of collective and State farms, and direct the development of each farm individually ... One must create agricultural administrative organs which would deal with planning, accounting and reporting, and which would influence the organisation of production on every farm. Without this one cannot manage agriculture.'[63]

The proposed organ was the 'territorial production directorate', to take charge of groups of collective and State farms throughout the country. A decree of March 22, 1962, introducing the reform, said the directorates' 'entire activity should be aimed at increasing agricultural output so as to ensure without fail the fulfilment of State purchasing plans and the creation of the necessary State reserves and funds in collective and State farms'.[64]

The directorates, said Khrushchev, should be 'formed out of the staff of [local] agricultural and procurement organs, party and soviet organisations'.[65] The reform meant, therefore, a large-scale reshuffling of local agricultural officials. It also involved the dismantling of the whole structure of procurement committees and Ministries which had been established with much fanfare only a year before. ('We have set up a large, qualified apparatus in the procurements system, but such large apparatuses are not needed for the purposes of procurement ... Should the Procurement Committee be preserved or should its functions be handed over to the production directorates?'[66] In fact, all the Procurement Committees and Ministries were now abolished, with the exception of the All-Union Committee.)[67]

Another confusing aspect of the reform was that it left vague the extent of the area and the number of farms to be covered by each directorate, though Khrushchev insisted that the area should overlap the existing *raion* administrative units, because if it coincided with them the directorates 'will degenerate into *raion* departments of agriculture, which we have abandoned' [since the reform of the Ministry of Agriculture].[68] The overlapping of local authorities which this caused, particularly the clash between *raion* party Secretaries and party officials in the directorates, was almost impossible to correct.

The directorates were headed by a director, had their own 'party organisers' assisted by two or three 'instructors', and were represented directly on the farms by 'inspector-organisers' (one for every four to six farms, for example, in the Ukraine).[69] A whole hierarchy of new Agricultural Committees was established to supervise the directorates. It was headed by an All-Union Committee for Agriculture, presided over by a deputy chairman of the USSR Council of Ministers and including the main party and government officials responsible for agriculture. Below came similar committees at republic level, where new Ministries for the production and procurement of agricultural products were set up, and at *oblast/krai* level. All these committees were presided over by the appropriate party First Secretary.

Only a few months later, at the November, 1962, plenum, the administrative structure was altered yet again. This meeting marked the high-point of Khrushchev's obsession with the need to bring party officials 'closer to the decisive sectors of production'.[70] It reorganised the party structure 'on the production principle', splitting it into two branches, one concerned with industry and the other with agriculture. The main party levers—the soviets, the trade unions and the Komsomol—were similarly bifurcated. The rural party *raikoms* were abolished and replaced by party committees in the production directorates.

The upheaval seems to have contributed nothing to the efficient running of agriculture. It disrupted traditional organisational patterns and the careers of party *apparatchiki* throughout the USSR. Its unpopularity in party circles was shown by the fact that it was the first of Khrushchev's reforms to be dismantled after his fall in November, 1964.

(c) PRESSURE ON THE PRIVATE PLOT

The post-Stalin régime's 1953 promise to relax pressure on the *kolkhozniks'* private plots and livestock was not kept. On the contrary, Khrushchev increased pressure by various indirect means. Thus, the ostensibly liberal decree of March 6, 1956, authorising *kolkhozes* to fix the size of private plots and livestock holdings, was used as the starting point for a campaign to reduce them. Much publicity was given to exemplary *kol-khozes* in which the *kolkhozniks* supposedly took the initiative in deciding on reductions. The campaign was particularly relentless in 1959, when *kolkhozniks'* cattle holdings fell by 13 per cent and their private plot areas by seven per cent.[71] Khrushchev helped it along by extolling *kolkhozniks* in his home village of Kalinovka who had sold their cattle to the *kolkhoz*.

He also began to squeeze out the *kolkhoz* markets. A decree of February, 1961,[72] noted that 'many *kolkhozniks* are diverted from *kolkhoz* production in order to travel, often long distances, to *kolkhoz* markets. This leads to considerable expenditure of time and labour.' The decree ordered the development of sales of surplus agricultural produce through the consumer co-operative network. In this way, 'the *kolkhozniks* will be spared the need to transport surpluses over great distances... and will not be distracted from production on the *kolkhozes*'. It was later revealed that more ruthless measures were applied: 'In many *raions* and *oblasts*, the hours and days when *kolkhoz* markets were open were reduced, the allocation of money for their construction and repair was stopped, and in places the markets were even closed... In the Press, the complete winding-up of *kolkhoz* trade was foretold and the fixing of firm prices in *kolkhoz* markets by administrative order, etc.'[73]

Despite these pressures, the private plots were still the main source of livelihood for many *kolkhozniks* at the end of the Khrushchev period.

'In many *kolkhozes* of the non-black-earth zone the basic guaranteed source of livelihood for the *kolkhoz* family remains even now the private plot. Moreover, a unit of labour expended on the private plot, as a rule, is more remunerative than a unit of labour expended on communal production.'[74]

THE FALL OF KHRUSHCHEV

Khrushchev was still busy with plans for reorganising the administration of agriculture when he was removed from power. A further plenum to discuss agriculture was scheduled for November, 1964, and Khrushchev had let it be known that he would present ideas for a further administrative reorganisation to allow more specialisation in individual branches of agriculture.[75] It could be that the need to forestall another of his

[66]

'hare-brained' agricultural schemes precipitated his downfall, but the failure of his agricultural policy was certainly one of the major factors in his eclipse. This failure had been made painfully clear by the extremely unpopular increase in retail prices for butter (25 per cent) and meat and meat products (30 per cent) in June, 1962,[76] and by the disastrous grain harvest of 1963 which necessitated the import of more than 9 million tons of grain worth about $800 million by the end of September, 1963.[77] Perhaps the most telling official admission of the failure to secure any permanent basic improvement in agricultural production since Stalin's death appeared in the party journal, *Kommunist*, in February, 1964. This pointed out that the value of agricultural production had not increased in the five years after 1958, while that of industrial production had risen by 58 per cent.

'The fact is that not a single branch of the economy can develop normally if the country lacks grain. Consequently the disproportion between industry and agriculture, which developed before 1953 and which was successfully being overcome in 1953 to 1958 . . . may now once again exert its negative influence on the development of industry and the national economy.'[78]

SOURCES

1. *Pravda*, December 17, 1953.
2. *Pravda*, February 9, 1955.
3. *Voprosi Istorii*, 1957, No. 5.
4. Plenum, p. 104.
5. KPSS, Vol. 2, pp. 1154–5.
6. *Pravda*, August 9, 1953.
7. Karcz and Timoshenko, p. 135.
8. *Pravda*, September 15, 1953 (Khrushchev).
9. *Pravda*, August 9, 1953.
10. Decree of August 8, 1953 (IKP Vol. 2, p. 352)
11. *Selskoe Khozyaistvo*, July 10, 1954.
12. *Pravda*, September 15, 1953.
13. KPSS, Vol. 2, p. 1195.
14. 'Delivery prices for many of the basic agricultural products (grains, animal products, potatoes, vegetables, etc.) were fixed basically in 1928–9, and remained practically without alteration until 1953'. Koravyakovsky, p. 87.
15. Karcz and Timoshenko, p. 134.
16. Korovyakovsky, p. 80.
17. *Pravda*, March 21, 1954.
18. *Pravda*, March 6, 1962; Karcz and Timoshenko, p. 130.
19. For example, in 1954–5, almost two-thirds of all graduates from agricultural institutes in the Ukraine were dispatched to the Virgin Lands. Dvoskin and Sidorov, p. 29.
20. Plenum, pp. 8, 46.
21. ES Kh, 1967, No. 7, p. 39.

22. *Ibid.*
23. Speech of January 25, 1955 (*Pravda*, February 3, 1955).
24. Ezhevsky told the March, 1965, plenum that the maize area had reached 34 million hectares. This information was greeted by 'noisy animation in the hall' (Plenum, p. 149). According to *Pravda*, March 5, 1965, the maize area had reached 37 million hectares.
25. *Pravda*, March 11, 1955.
26. *Pravda*, April 5, 1955.
27. Plenum, pp. 144–5. Towards the end of the Khrushchev régime a decree of March 20, 1964 (*Pravda*, March 23, 1964), admitted that the new planning system was not being adhered to, and that production and crop plans were 'unceremoniously' imposed on the farms. But this was blamed on local officials.
28. *Pravda*, March 10, 1956.
29. *Selskoe Khozyaistvo*, July 10, 1954.
30. A separate decree of March 6, 1956, made provision for this, and fixed the proportion of *kolkhoz* income to be used for advances (25 per cent of income and 50 per cent of advances from procurement agencies). *Pravda*, March 10, 1956.
31. Plenum, pp. 27, 47.
32. *Pravda*, January 25, 1958.
33. *Pravda*, December 16, 1958.
34. *Pravda*, March 1, 1958.
35. *Pravda*, April 1, 1958.
36. *Pravda*, July 14, 1959.
37. SIE, Vol. 9, p. 207.
38. *Pravda*, March 1, 1958.
39. *Ibid.*
40. *Voprosi Ekonomiki*, 1965, No. 6, p. 5 (Matskevich).
41. Plenum, p. 218.
42. *Ibid.*, pp. 177, 216–17; *Voprosi Ekonomiki*, 1965, No. 6, pp. 5–6.
43. Decree of June 24, 1954 (*Pravda*, June 27, 1954).
44. Decree of July 4, 1957 (*Pravda*, July 5, 1957).
45. *Pravda*, June 20, 1958.
46. The 'per hectare principle' was supposed to ensure equal obligations for farms having equal climatic, soil and other conditions; but was usually ignored in practice, because local authorities arbitrarily increased the obligations of the more successful farms in order to offset under-fulfilment of obligations by other farms in the same district. KPSS, Vol. 2, p. 1156; *Pravda*, March 6, 1954, and February 3, 1955.
47. *Pravda*, June 21, 1958.
48. *Ibid.*
49. *Ibid.*
50. Plenum, pp. 7–9.
51. *Ibid.*, p. 10.
52. *Ibid.*, p. 74.
53. *Vestnik Statistiki*, 1965, No. 8, p. 14.
54. *Pravda*, January 14, 1961, and January 22, 1961.
55. *Pravda*, January 14, 1961.
56. Matskevich was replaced by Olshansky in December, 1960; Olshansky by Pysin in April, 1962; and Pysin by Volovchenko in March, 1963.
57. *Pravda*, February 21, 1961.
58. *Ibid.*
59. *Pravda*, January 21, 1961.
60. *Pravda*, February 26, 1961.
61. *Ibid.*
62. *Pravda*, March 6, 1962.

63. *Ibid.*
64. *Pravda*, March 24, 1962.
65. *Pravda*, March 6, 1962.
66. *Ibid.*
67. Decree of March 22, 1962 (*Pravda*, March 24, 1962).
68. *Pravda*, March 6, 1962. It was stated later that in the RSFSR each Directorate would control an average of 30 to 60 farms. Elsewhere the average might be as low as 15 or as high as 100 farms (*Kolkhoznoe Pravo*, p. 166). Voronov said that in the RSFSR each directorate would comprise an average of five to ten *raions*; Podgorny said in the Ukraine the average would be three *raions* (*Pravda*, March 7, 1962).
69. *Pravda*, March 7, 1962 (Podgorny).
70. *Pravda*, September 15, 1953.
71. *New Directions*, p. 414 (Karcz).
72. *Pravda*, February 26, 1961.
73. *Voprosi Ekonomiki*, 1962, No. 2, p. 62.
74. Plenum, p. 176.
75. *Pravda*, August 10 and 12, 1964.
76. *Pravda*, June 1, 1962.
77. *Pravda*, October 2, 1963.
78. *Kommunist*, 1964, No. 2, pp. 8–9.

III
The Post-Khrushchev Period

(a) THE 1965 REFORMS

The post-Khrushchev régime, like that which followed Stalin's death, found that agriculture presented the most pressing problems and they were the first to claim its attention. The first important Central Committee plenum[1] in March, 1965, heard Brezhnev report on 'urgent measures for the development of agriculture'.

As in 1953, the opportunity was taken of dissociating the new leaders from mistakes admitted to have been made in the past, and of encouraging the idea that a fresh start would be made and a new and happier chapter opened in Soviet farm policy. This time, however, the admissions of past errors and existing shortcomings were much franker, and the agricultural situation as a whole was treated with greater realism.

The suggested remedies were essentially similar to those proposed in 1953. The main elements of the programme were:

(a) increased agricultural investment;

(b) concessions to the peasants; as in 1953, these comprised price increases and quota reductions for compulsory deliveries—with the innovation that grain delivery quotas were pegged at the same level for five years; the mitigation of restrictions on private plots and livestock, reduced taxation, and the remission of debts;

(c) the restructuring of political and administrative controls.

INVESTMENTS

The need for greater agricultural investment was one of the main themes of the March, 1965, plenum. Brezhnev cited the decline in investments towards the end of the Khrushchev period as one of the main reasons for the decline in agricultural performance. He pointed out that its share of the total national investment declined from 11·3 per cent in 1954–8 to a planned 7·5 per cent in 1959–65.[2]

Other speakers strongly pressed the needs of agriculture. Zolotukhin, First Secretary of the Tambov *obkom*, said:

'Year after year financial, material and technical aid [to the farms] was cut, and the attempt was made to pump as many resources as possible out of agriculture. The urgent measures with which we are now concerned should indeed consist primarily in altering our very policy and approach to agriculture, in correctly understanding its needs, and in doing away with our habitual underestimation of agriculture in the national economy.'[3]

Nuriev, First Secretary of the Bashkir *obkom*, put it more bluntly:

'Large sums in capital investment are required for the improvement of agriculture, otherwise it will continue to be our Achilles' heel . . . We should long ago have ceased the practice of solving all our difficulties at the expense of the interests of agriculture . . . It is inadmissible that there should be such a large gap in supplying State and collective farms with their elementary requirements for machines, mechanical equipment, transport, fertilisers, and herbicides.'[4]

Brezhnev proposed that State and collective farm investments in agriculture should total 71 milliard roubles during 1966–70[5]—41 milliard to be provided by the State and 30 milliard by the collective farms. State investments would be roughly twice what they had been during the previous five years. This was an ambitious but not unprecedented proposal. Khrushchev had, in fact, succeeded in doubling agricultural investment in the 1954–8 period compared with 1950–3. Nevertheless, doubts about its feasibility and its sponsors' ability to ensure its implementation were raised soon after, when Brezhnev told the September, 1965, plenum:

'I must point out that in some sectors of our State apparatus . . . the tendency to improve other matters, to "balance the books", at the expense of agriculture, to infringe the interests of collective and State farms, has not yet been eliminated. And this occurs despite the very clear decisions at the March plenum calling for maximum aid to agriculture.'[6]

Liberal economists openly said that investment was still inadequate. 'Agriculture continues to receive from the national economy less than is necessary',[7] wrote V. Venzher in March,

1966. But resistance to the increased investment appears to have been strengthened by the bumper harvest of 1966, just as a similar situation in 1958 appears to have tempted Khrushchev into economising on agriculture.

Polyansky, the Politburo member responsible for agriculture, revealed that there was serious dissension over this issue:

'We must resolutely see to it that capital investments and material resources are used strictly as allocated and with maximum effectiveness. This has to be mentioned because . . . some comrades are beginning to argue that collective and State farms can now develop even with less substantial aid, that we can now cut down the scale of land improvement works and reduce deliveries to agriculture of machinery and mineral fertiliser. Such arguments are harmful. They must be decisively suppressed.'[8]

Baibakov, chairman of *Gosplan*, confirmed in a speech to the Supreme Soviet in October, 1967,[9] that planned agricultural investments were 'unfortunately still not being fulfilled', and gave figures implying that actual investments were running about 30 per cent below the level planned in March, 1965. He announced that capital investment in the national economy as a whole was being cut by two per cent compared with the Five-Year Plan directives agreed in 1966, and gave a figure indicating that the cut would particularly affect State investments in agriculture, reducing them by 13 per cent compared with the March, 1965, target.

Polyansky, however, seemed determined to continue his public defence of what now appeared to be a losing cause. In a striking article in *Kommunist*[10] (published on the eve of the 50th anniversary of the October Revolution, when care was generally being taken to avoid raising controversial matters) he argued for 'more correct proportions between industry and agriculture', and emphasised that 'Socialist industry cannot develop by weakening agriculture'. He stressed that agriculture was still being starved of machinery and electric power ('many operations are even now still carried out by hand. The level of electric power resources in agriculture per worker is still below the level in the more developed capitalist countries . . . Even such a labour-consuming process as milking is done approximately two-thirds by hand.') But his strongest card was to quote Brezhnev's warning at the September, 1965, plenum against 'balancing the books' at the expense of agriculture. He added that Brezhnev had said: 'Such tendencies are very dangerous for our common cause', and had given this warning 'more than once'.

Clearly, there can be no certainty about the development of agriculture, or conditions for agricultural workers, while the investment level remains a matter of dispute.

CONCESSIONS

i. Private Plots

The post-Khrushchev régime's first significant act after Khrushchev's fall was to lift restrictions which he had imposed on private plots and livestock. Such a concession was apparently felt to be too urgent to await the March, 1965, plenum (on 'urgent measures for the development of agriculture').

Brezhnev reportedly won a round of applause when he declared in a speech of November 6, 1964: 'In recent years, unjustified limitations have been imposed in this sphere [the private plot economy], although the economic conditions were not ripe for such a step. These limitations have now been removed.'[11] Shelest, the Ukrainian party leader, had revealed in *Pravda* the day before, that 'recently party organisations in the Ukraine have been taking steps to help *kolkhozniks*, workers and employees to possess privately, if they want to, a certain number of cattle, pigs, sheep and poultry. The other day, the Ukrainian party Central Committee and Council of Ministers passed a decision rescinding the unjustified limitations imposed several years ago on the private plots of *kolhozniks* ...'[12]

Summaries of the Ukrainian decree and of similar ones in other Republics were published,[13] but without revealing the extent of the restrictions to be removed, vouchsafing merely that they had been imposed 'after 1955' (i.e. presumably under the pretext of applying the decree of March 6, 1956 (*see* Section II, pp. 58, 65–6).

Restrictions were also lifted from the *kolkhoz* 'free' market. In particular, the practice of imposing ceiling prices on marketed produce was forbidden. Funds were ordered to be made available for the construction and repair of markets. Railway station and river landing markets (informal, traditional arrangements) were permitted, and the transport Militia was told to stop breaking them up.[14]

In practice, many of the restrictions on private plots imposed under Khrushchev persisted under his successors, despite their supposed abolition. A year after the decree rescinding them in the RSFSR, another decree was issued which admitted that in many *oblasts* private plots had still not been restored to their rightful size. On the contrary, further improper reductions were being made in the plots of certain *kolkhozniks* such as the unmarried, the elderly and those receiving a pension. Moreover, compulsory deliveries of meat, milk, eggs, wool, etc., were being extracted from *kolkhozniks*, in direct contravention of the decree of July 4, 1957 (*see* Section II, p. 60), exempting them from such deliveries. *Kolkhozniks* were not only not receiving any encouragement to market the produce of their plots, but were actively prevented from doing so.[15]

ii. Procurements

The main stimulus to production devised by the March, 1965, plenum was the reform of the procurement price and quota system. Prices were raised—for wheat and rye by an average of 12 per cent; for meat by 36 per cent[16]—and the system of premium prices for above-quota grain deliveries, abolished in 1958, was reintroduced. The latter were fixed at 50 per cent above the basic price for wheat, rye and other grains. The price increases for livestock products, it was subsequently made clear, were regarded as temporary subsidies.[17] The new prices, Brezhnev claimed, would make grain growing profitable even in marginal grain areas such as Belorussia and the Baltic Republics.[18] He did not make a similar claim for the new livestock prices, and it was later admitted that production costs (based on the meat-feed ratio) in many farms in Belorussia and Georgia 'are so high that even the increased procurement prices will not cover them'.[19] More recently, *Pravda* reported that livestock farming in the Ukraine was still only barely profitable (1·7 per cent in 1966, two per cent in 1967), and that 'in many farms' it brought a loss.[20]

Procurement quotas for grain were reduced by 15 per cent compared with the already approved plan for 1965 (but remained 7·9 per cent above the actual level of 1960–4), and were fixed at this level for the remainder of the Five Year Plan, up to and including 1970. Brezhnev admitted that this level 'will not entirely satisfy the growing demands of the country, nor permit the creation of government reserves',[21] but implied that the gap would be comfortably filled by above-quota deliveries (which would therefore have to increase year by year). Although above-quota deliveries are supposedly voluntary, there remains a large element of compulsion in them. Indeed, the yearly contracts between the farms and the procurement agencies for quota deliveries may also specify the above-quota deliveries, although the farms try to resist this, fearing that the penalties for not fulfilling above-quota deliveries will be the same as those for under-fulfilment of the quota plan.[22] According to one Soviet economist, there is in practice no difference between quota and above-quota deliveries except the price, and 'the principle that the *kolkhozes* may freely dispose of their surplus to plan produce will not find its full expression for several years to come'.[23]

Although Brezhnev stressed the advantages for the farms of having firm grain quotas for several years ahead (which 'no one has the right to alter'[24]), they seem to have been altered soon after the March, 1965, plenum and slightly reduced, in response to claims that they were still too high.[25] In any case, if the above-quota deliveries are, in practice, just as obligatory as the quotas, and are altered every year (upwards), the farms remain with the same uncertainty about the extent of their delivery obligation as before.

Quotas for livestock produce were also reduced but, unlike those for grain, were planned to rise throughout the Five-Year Plan.

iii. Financial Concessions

Kolkhoz incomes and peasant living standards, which had risen in the first years of Khrushchev, declined or stagnated after 1958. According to Matskevich, USSR Minister of Agriculture, *kolkhoz incomes* 'declined on the one hand as a result of the reduction of prices for their produce, and on the other as a result of an increase in prices of industrial goods used by the *kolkhozes*' (tractors, trucks, spares, fuel).[26]

Florentev, RSFSR Minister of Agriculture, pleaded eloquently at the March, 1965, plenum for the increased investments in agriculture to be used for raising living standards:

'If this most important side of the matter is lost sight of, the increased capital investments in agriculture may not produce the required return in increased production. As you know, this happened more than once before.'[27]

In addition to the higher prices for agricultural produce, the March, 1965, plenum offered the peasants a series of financial concessions to boost incomes. They included: a reform of the *kolkhoz* income tax, which it was claimed would halve the tax burden[28] (the tax to be paid on net instead of gross income, and at a rate of 12 per cent only on that portion which exceeded a profitability rate of 15 per cent)[29]; large-scale cancellation or deferment of debts, including those for the purchase of MTS machinery[30]; a reduction, starting in 1966, of prices for farm vehicles, machinery, spares and electricity[31]; the gradual institution of direct credits from the State Bank (instead of *via* the procurement agencies) to cover seasonal monetary deficits, including cash wages to agricultural workers[32]; and the abolition of the surcharge on consumer goods sold in rural areas.[33]

ORGANISATIONAL REFORMS

The new régime, in November, 1964, unified the structure of the party apparatus,[34] restoring to it the pattern which had been traditional before Khrushchev divided it in November, 1962, into industrial and agricultural segments. In particular, the authorities restored the vital lower link—the rural *raikoms* [*raion* party Committees], which had been replaced by party Committees in the territorial production directorates. The Ministry of Agriculture, which had been deprived of its policy and executive functions in 1961, had them restored. A decree of March 1, 1965,[35] made the Ministry once more directly responsible for State and collective farms and transformed the territorial production directorates, established in March, 1962, into the Ministry's local organs of control—renamed 'agricultural production directorates'.

Shortly before the March, 1965, plenum, Matskevich, who had run the Ministry with considerable success in the early Khrushchev period (1955–60) was reappointed Minister.[36] At the beginning of 1965, the Ministry moved its offices back to Moscow.[37]

Brezhnev promised at the March, 1965, plenum that greater respect would be paid to the principles of '*kolkhoz* democracy', which he confessed had been 'grossly infringed' in the past. ('In many *kolkhozes*, the bulk of the members are in practice excluded from the discussion and decision of the most important questions'.)[38] But his main proposal in this context—the

[76]

holding of a *kolkhozniks'* Congress to approve new *kolkhoz* Statutes[39] has so far not materialised, though there has been desultory discussion in the Press and at conferences on how the Statutes might be improved; and a drafting commission, headed by Brezhnev, with a membership of 149 (mostly senior party officials), was set up in January, 1966.[40]

Brezhnev also indicated that the process of merging *kolkhozes* or transforming them into State farms, which Khrushchev had sponsored, would be halted, and that 'at the present stage it is not our duty to hasten the transformation of one form [of farm] into the other, but to assist in every possible way the development and flourishing of both types of communal farming'.[41] Since the end of 1964, the growth in the number of State farms and decline in the number of collective farms seems to have halted.

AGRICULTURAL SCIENCE

One of the earliest consequences of Khrushchev's fall was the final discrediting of Academician Lysenko, who for many years, under the protection first of Stalin and then of Khrushchev, had succeeded in foisting his idiosyncratic ideas on Soviet agriculture and biological science. Less than a week after his patron's fall,[42] Lysenko and his doctrines were attacked in the Press. For the first time, details emerged of the damage he and his followers had caused since the mid-'thirties in various fields of science (by rejecting the results of modern research, both foreign and Soviet), in education (by distorting the teaching of biology), in health ('the fact that a doctor graduating from a Soviet medical school has almost no idea about heredity leads to shortcomings in diagnosing and treating inherited disorders')[43] and, not least, in farming.

Examples of the latter were his insistence on sowing winter rye on stubble in the Virgin Lands in the autumn of 1962, half of which perished; his opposition to hybrid maize, which caused 'colossal damage'[44]; his insistence on sowing winter wheat on stubble in Siberia in 1941–4 ('the grain, as might have been expected, was killed by frost')[45]; and his experimental crossing of Jersey cows with other breeds, which led only to the destruction of decades of work by other scientists in building up cattle breeds.[46]

Even before the March, 1965, plenum, it was evident that

[77]

the agricultural cropping patterns imposed by Khrushchev would not be retained. A group of agricultural scientists described in *Pravda*[47] how, 'contrary to ... biological principles for the siting of crops, maize was pushed far to the north and east', and deplored that 'in many areas of the country grasses were almost entirely ousted'. Matskevich subsequently stated that 'great damage' had been caused by the imposition, by administrative order, of 'miracle crops' and 'miracle methods', and said that 'measures for restoring crop rotations which were upset during recent years in many farms and even whole zones' would be taken.[48]

(b) CURRENT CONTROVERSIES

The post-Khrushchev period has been marked by the sporadic but persistent airing of a number of unresolved controversies over agricultural reform.

The most important of these concerns proposals to give farms greater freedom from centralised State control, particularly in the planning and marketing of their produce, and to provide greater scope for market forces, rather in the spirit of Professor Liberman's proposals for the reform of industry.

PLANNING AND MARKETING

Defects in planning and procurement methods were a point of discussion before the March, 1965, plenum on agriculture. Economists had urged the need to give farms more say in planning their production, and to combine planning 'from above' with planning 'from below'.[49] L. Kassirov, writing in *Pravda* in January, 1965, urged that profit should be the sole criterion for evaluating the work of any farm. The unwieldy and administrative character of the planned assignments, he said, hindered the development of initiative. He recommended that the plan should be drawn up on the basis of proposals worked out by the farms themselves, as they were best able to determine what could rationally be produced.[50]

It was evident soon after the plenum that the reforms which it introduced had not gone far enough in the eyes of the more liberal economists, who reiterated the proposal that farms should formulate their own production plans. M. Lemeshev also advocated that they should be free to buy their own machinery and fertilisers directly from the factories, and have greater scope to sell surplus produce on local markets.[51]

Even more strikingly formulated and persuasively argued were the proposals of G. Lisichkin, in the 'liberal' journal, *Novy Mir*, in September, 1965.[52] He urged that 'farm workers should take the most direct part in deciding such vitally important questions as the planning of their production, the marketing of the produce grown by them, the regulation of prices for it and the obtaining of the equipment necessary for production'. He suggested that compulsory deliveries should be replaced by 'genuinely free contracting for all products'. He argued:

'At first sight, such a proposal will seem to many simply blasphemous—after all, Socialist planning in agriculture is usually associated with the system of giving planned tasks to collective and State farms. But to those who think thus, one may say that planning of that kind was "invented" long before its present zealous defenders were born. In 1914–16 in Russia plans for the production and sale of grain at stable State prices were also given to the *uyezds* (Tsarist provinces). Planning by issuing directives is much less effective than genuine economic planning ... We are not, therefore, against planning, but for a different methodology of planning ... Planning by means of economic levers requires special attention to the price mechanism. Prices must not be arrived at by administrative procedure, though administrative organs may fix them.'

Kassirov returned to the attack with more detailed proposals in *Problems of Economics* in January, 1966.[53] The farms, he said, should have planned for them only the total value of their deliveries, and be left to decide themselves which products they would contract to deliver to the procurement agencies in order to fulfil this purely monetary plan. The procurement agencies, not the farms, would have to fulfil plans for securing agricultural deliveries by volume and type of product. If the volume or pattern of deliveries appeared to be developing unsatisfactorily for the State's requirements, the flow would be regulated 'not by administrative but by economic methods', by adjusting prices.

During the first half of 1966, the reform movement seemed to be gathering strength, and numerous articles in its support appeared in the Press.[54] Perhaps the most influential reinforcement came from the economist V. G. Venzher, well known for having earned a rebuff from Stalin for proposing the abolition of the MTS in October, 1953 (*see* Section I, p. 45). He spoke of the 'fruitful peaceful competition' which would be engendered among the farms by the development of market relations.[55] Both Venzher and Lisichkin published books expounding and defending the need for the reform of planning and marketing.[56]

It was not until the autumn of 1966 that the forces of orthodoxy mounted a counter-attack. A long article in the agricultural newspaper, *Selskaya Zhizn*, by three economists, said that the proposed reforms, if put into effect, 'could damage the further development of agriculture and the whole national economy'.[57] The reformers were accused of 'pressing for the revision of the principles of planning the Socialist economy worked out at the March and September [1965] plenums of the CPSU Central Committee'.

A spate of similar condemnatory articles followed.[58] But nowhere was there a serious or detailed examination of the reformers' arguments. A *Pravda* editorial on March 4, 1967, delivered what the orthodox camp no doubt hoped would be the *coup de grâce*: 'The views of certain economists who propose to do away with the assignment of firm plans to the farms for the sale of produce to the State or to plan their targets only in monetary terms are clearly mistaken. These proposals are in fact calculated to weaken centralised planning. Their adoption could only harm the development of Socialist agriculture.'

But Lisichkin could not be silenced so easily. In an issue of *Novy Mir*,[59] signed for publication only two days after *Pravda*'s denunciation of his views, he put out a forcible restatement of them and attacked his critics for deliberately misrepresenting his arguments so as to make them seem foolish and irresponsible.

Throughout 1967, the reformists' views continued to be the subject of Press criticism. Towards the end of the year, a collection of articles by party and government officials and agricultural economists, headed by Matskevich, Minister of Agriculture, was published as a book, *Results and Prospects— Agriculture after the March Plenum of the CPSU.CC*. It was in fact a concerted attack on the reformists. The most serious charges levelled against them were that they were challenging recently-formulated party policy ('pressing for the revision of the principles of planning the Socialist economy worked out at the March and September [1965] plenums of the CPSU.CC'),[60] and that their ideas would subvert the whole economy ('lead inevitably to the emergence of a great imbalance between industry and agriculture, a rise in prices of agricultural produce, and speculation in it, to difficulties in supplying urban and industrial centres with food and raw materials, and to the dislocation of the entire national economy').[61]

An even greater degree of official disapproval was expressed when Polyansky, the Politburo member in charge of agriculture, declared in an article in *Kommunist*[62] that the reformists were 'grossly in error'. 'Some economists', he wrote, 'go so far as to say that planned targets contradict the nature of the *kolkhoz* system. This is sheer nonsense.'

Still Lisichkin was not abashed. At the end of the 1967, he published a further article in *Novy Mir*,[63] which, while ignoring the high-level expressions of displeasure at his views, demolished some of his minor detractors in *Selskaya Zhizn*. He demonstrated that 'instead of proving their case with effective arguments they try to intimidate their adversaries by baseless accusations'. This retort, by implication, applied equally to *Pravda* and Polyansky.

According to Lisichkin, 'our opponents are afraid of free marketing of produce, because they see in it the danger of anarchy and disorder'.[64] Though it serves the critics' purpose to exaggerate the possible consequences of the proposed reform, it seems probable that their basic objection is indeed fear that it would open the way to a progressive collapse of the régime's hold on the economy. The objection is thus political rather than economic. The régime and the orthodox economists are doubtless well aware of all the disadvantages in agriculture arising from the existing 'command-economy' system, against which the reformers inveigh, but prefer to continue accepting them rather than tamper with the system. They are not prepared to contemplate any significant shift in decision-making from the centre to the farms, even though the latter are staffed and controlled by political appointees.

'LINKS'

Another controversy, on a more narrow issue, concerns the organisation of labour in *kolkhozes*—specifically the rôle of the 'link' or 'squad'.

This is an old controversy with roots in the Stalin era (*see* Section I, pp. 38, 43–4). The link system was devised in the 1930s as a method of overcoming the chronic apathy and lack of personal responsibility which plagued the *kolkhozes*. It involved assigning a portion of the *kolkoz* land and machinery to small teams or links of perhaps six or seven workers who were given charge of farming operations over a lengthy period. The system was encouraged until 1950, when it was suddenly denounced, apparently because Stalin felt it took the devolution of responsibility too far and threatened to disintegrate the *kolkhozes*.

Khrushchev, especially during his later years, experimented with various kinds of links. A Central Committee plenum in June 1954, condemned 'underestimation' of the links, and said they should be encouraged in the cultivation of row and technical crops.[65] After the transfer of machinery from the MTS to the *kolkhozes*, from 1958 onwards, there was a great increase in 'mechanised links'. These were sometimes much bigger than the traditional links, and were used for a greater variety of tasks, especially maize cultivation. Khrushchev was alive to the danger that the system might be used to restore a disguised form of individual peasant farming—as was clear from occasional denunciations of cases in which work, land and equipment had been assigned to individual families instead of to production teams.[66]

Soon after Khrushchev's fall, the links issue was taken up by *Komsomolskaya Pravda*. Experiments in self-accounting mechanised links in State farms in the Virgin Lands and the Altai were said to have met with bureaucratic opposition, despite the fact that they had shown that the system could do a lot to improve poor labour morale and incentives.[67] A subsequent article, by a combine driver in Kazakhstan, went much further. After disclaiming any desire to become 'a private land-owner', he continued: 'But I would like to be in a link. A plot of *sovkhoz* or *kolkhoz* land should be assigned to several families. And our earnings should depend on what we give the State from this land'.[68]

The most detailed proposals for making the farm-worker a real 'master of the land' came in August, 1965, from Zhulin, an agronomist in the Altai. Land should be allocated to links for several years, he recommended, and the allocation should be on a proper legal basis, not merely on a verbal understanding. The link would then be 'a legally independent production unit with corresponding rights and duties'; land would be entrusted to 'a group of persons with the right to be its master in the name of and on behalf of the people'.[69]

Komsomolskaya Pravda continued to champion the link system against economists, agricultural scientists and officials who viewed it 'with mistrust',[70] as 'not Socialist',[71] or as 'a lapse into property-owning'.[72] It was not until 1966 that approval, albeit lukewarm, was given for experiments with links in *Selskaya Zhizn*,[73] and then in *Pravda*,[74] which declared:

'Maybe everything in this experiment has not been worked out in detail, and perhaps there is something debatable in its methods, but the facts speak for themselves.'[75]

Despite *Pravda*'s intervention, conservative resistance to the experiments has continued. *Komsomolskaya Pravda* indignantly reported in May, 1967,[76] that the Ministry of Agriculture and the State Committee on Labour and Wages had 'done nothing to support the movement', and that their negative attitude had 'led to the dissolution of many mechanised links bereft of moral and organisational support'. And six months later the newspaper had to regret that this and previous protests had elicited no action from the appropriate authorities.[77]

The party leadership apparently prefers to let the desultory discussion of this issue continue indefinitely rather than make its mind up about it.

KOLKHOZ UNIONS

Unlike the controversies over planning, marketing and links, that over *kolkhoz* unions was brought to the fore by the party leadership—by Brezhnev's suggestion at the March, 1966, Party Congress that elective *kolkhoz* unions, which had existed from *raion* to all-union level in the early period of collectivisation, might be resurrected.

Brezhnev alleged that in their time the unions had been 're-garded as authoritative by the peasants', and had 'allowed the collective farm system to be further democratised and the broad masses of *kolkhozniks* to be drawn into economic, cultural and social activity'.[78] In fact, they had only a brief and shadowy existence after 1929, and were completely submerged in the turmoil of mass collectivisation, and finally abolished in 1932.[79]

Khrushchev had toyed with the idea of re-establishing the

unions after the abolition of the MTS in 1958.[80] The matter was raised again at the December, 1959, Central Committee plenum, at which a considerable divergence of opinion on it emerged. Khrushchev said they should think only about establishing *raion kolkhoz* unions—it was too early to set up a central organisation for them.[81] Matskevich, then as now Minister of Agriculture, was also against any 'independent system' of unions above *raion* level.[82] Polyansky, then Chairman of the RSFSR Council of Ministers, pushed the idea furthest. He favoured *raion, oblast* and Republic unions, which would 'take on themselves the functions of operative control of the *kolkhozes*'.[83] He pointed out this would entail a reorganisation of the Ministry of Agriculture and substantial reduction of its work. The final resolution of the plenum merely instructed the party Presidium to study the matter further.[84]

With the creation of territorial production administrations in March, 1962, the question of *kolkhoz* unions was by-passed. The new administrations took over the management of the inter-*kolkhoz* construction and other organisations, which had considerably expanded, and some of which had created their own hierarchical systems.

In the post-Khrushchev period, the issue of *kolkhoz* unions was raised again in the course of the Press discussion of possible amendments to the *kolkhoz* Statutes, which the March, 1965, plenum had agreed would be revised at a forthcoming *Kolkhozniks'* Congress. Those who favoured the unions stressed both political and economic advantages which they might bring. The unions, it was urged, would 'defend the *kolkhozes'* interests in their relations with other organisations',[85] or facilitate the struggle against a high-handed attitude towards *kolkhozes* by certain representatives of State organs, and help to preserve the democratic bases of management in each individual *kolkhoz*'.[86] They would also, it was suggested, 'contribute to finally solving the problem of economically weak *kolkhozes*', since all the *kolkhozes* in a union would contribute to a common fund from which the weaker ones would benefit.[87] Objections to these arguments were also raised, especially to the suggestion that the economically strong *kolkhozes* should be made to rescue the weaker ones.[88]

When Brezhnev proposed the establishment of unions, at local levels and in the centre, at the March, 1966, Party Congress, it was in a tentative manner, evidently without wishing

[84]

to commit himself too much to the idea ('We should like to have your opinion as to whether it would be advisable to set up . . .').[89] The idea was briefly supported by Shelest, the Ukrainian party leader.[90] Matskevich's continued opposition to it was implied by the fact that he ignored the topic.[91] Kebin, the Estonian party leader, also indicated his opposition, by remarking that the *raion* production administrations (i.e., the Ministry of Agriculture) were 'the best organisational form for directing both *kolkhozes* and *sovkhozes*', and that there had already been 'more than enough experiments and reorganisations'.[92] The outcome, once again, was merely a recommendation that the matter be examined further.[93]

Since the Party Congress, the pros and cons of establishing unions have been further debated in the Press, but no decision on the matter appears in sight, especially with the continued postponement of the *Kolkhozniks'* Congress to which the question should be submitted.

SOURCES

1. A plenum of November 16, 1964, had ordered the undoing of Khrushchev's bifurcation of the party apparatus, and made personnel changes.
2. Plenum, p. 8.
3. *Ibid.*, p. 53.
4. *Ibid.*, pp. 97–8.
5. *Ibid.*, p. 21.
6. *Pravda,* September 30, 1965.
7. *Komsomolskaya Pravda,* March 22, 1966.
8. *Pravda,* March 3, 1967.
9. *Pravda,* October 11, 1967.
10. *Kommunist,* 1967, No. 15.
11. *Pravda,* November 7, 1964.
12. *Pravda,* November 6, 1964.
13. *Pravda Ukrainy,* November 5, 1964; *Sovetskaya Rossiya,* November 14, 1964.
14. *Sovetskaya Rossiya,* May 13, 1965.
15. *Selskaya Zhizn,* November 4, 1965; *Kommunist,* 1965, No. 16, pp. 72–3.
16. Golikov, p. 37. The price for milk had been raised even before the plenum, by a decree of November 16, 1954 (*Spravochnik Partiinogo Rabotnika,* 1966, p. 149).
17. Zaslavskaya, p. 54.
18. Plenum, p. 11.
19. *Vestnik Statistiki,* 1965, No. 8, p. 16.
20. *Pravda,* February 3, 1968.
21. Plenum, p. 12.
22. *Selskaya Zhizn,* November 30, 1967; *Pravda Ukrainy,* December 16, 1967.
23. Zaslavskaya, p. 119.
24. Plenum, p. 18.
25. *Vestnik Statistiki,* 1965, No. 8, p. 17 gave the annual grain quota for 1965–70 as 53·1 million tons, instead of 55·749 million tons as fixed at the March, 1965, plenum and in a decree of April 1, 1965 (*Pravda,* April 12,

1965). Shelest, Pysin and Kunaev had expressed misgivings about the quotas for their Republics at the plenum (Plenum, pp. 40, 51, 101).

26. *Voprosi Ekonomiki*, 1965, No. 6, p. 5.

27. Plenum, p. 179.

28. *Selskaya Zhizn*, April 24, 1965.

29. Decree of April 10, 1965 (*Pravda*, April 11, 1965).

30. *Pravda*, April 20, 1965.

31. *Izvestiya*, December 25, 1965, and December 26, 1965.

32. *Izvestiya*, December 26, 1965.

33. This was not completed until January 1, 1966 (*Pravda*, December 31, 1965).

34. *Pravda*, November 17, 1964.

35. *Spravochnik Partiinogo Rabotnika*, 1966, p. 161.

36. *Pravda*, February 18, 1965.

37. *Pravda*, March 9, 1966.

38. Plenum, p. 28.

39. *Ibid.*, pp. 28, 237. The proposal to hold a Congress of *kolkhozniks* was not new. It had been put forward under Khrushchev, as long ago as February, 1958, when the Congress was scheduled for the beginning of 1959, but it never materialised (*Pravda*, February 28, 1958).

40. *Pravda*, January 26, 1966.

41. Plenum, p. 27.

42. *Komsomolskaya Pravda*, October 21, 1964, opened the attack with a denunciation of "dilettante experiments and hasty deductions" in livestock research.

43. *Komsomolskaya Pravda*, November 17, 1964.

44. *Literaturnaya Gazeta*, November 24, 1964.

45. *Sovetskaya Rossiya*, November 27, 1964.

46. *Komsomolskaya Pravda*, November 29, 1964.

47. *Pravda*, March 5, 1965.

48. *Bakinsky Rabochy*, April 4, 1965; *Selskaya Zhizn*, June 24, 1965.

49. *Ekonomicheskaya Gazeta*, February 17, 1965, pp. 2–3.

50. *Pravda*, January 22, 1965.

51. *Selskaya Zhizn*, July 3, 1965.

52. *Novy Mir*, 1965, No. 9, pp. 212–29.

53. *Voprosi Ekonomiki*, 1966, No. 1, pp. 37–46.

54. *Izvestiya*, February 25 and 27, 1966, March 12, 1966, April 19, 1966; *Pravda*, April 24, 1966; *Komsomolskaya Pravda*, March 17, 1966.

55. *Komsomolskaya Pravda*, March 22, 1966.

56. V. G. Venzher, 'The Kolkhoz system at the present stage', *Ekonomika* Publishing House, 1966; G. S. Lisichkin, 'Plan and Market', *Ekonomika*, 1966.

57. *Selskaya Zhizn*, September 22, 1966.

58. *Selskaya Zhizn*, November 29, December 8 and 21, 1966; and January 25 and February 28, 1967.

59. *Novy Mir*, 1967, No. 2, pp. 160–85.

60. Golikov, p. 190.

61. *Ibid.*, p. 148.

62. *Kommunist*, 1967, No. 15.

63. *Novy Mir*, 1967, No. 12, pp. 228–35.

64. *Novy Mir*, 1967, No. 2, p. 181.

65. *Pravda*, June 27, 1954.

66. *Kolkhoznoe Pravo,* p. 332.
67. *Komsomolskaya Pravda,* December 3, 1964.
68. *Komsomolskaya Pravda,* May 25, 1965.
69. *Komsomolskaya Pravda,* August 7, 1965.
70. *Komsomolskaya Pravda,* September 29, 1965.
71. *Komsomolskaya Pravda,* October 15, 1965.
72. *Ibid.*
73. *Selskaya Zhizn,* January 12, 1966.
74. *Pravda,* August 30, 1966.
75. *Pravda,* December 10, 1966.
76. *Komsomolskaya Pravda,* May 20, 1967.
77. *Komsomolskaya Pravda,* November 17, 1967.
78. *XXIII S'ezd KPSS,* Vol. 1, p. 68.
79. The history of the unions is dealt with in *Sovetskoe Gosudarstvo i Pravo,* 1967, No. 4, pp. 97–101.
80. *Pravda,* December 29, 1959.
81. *Ibid.*
82. *Pravda,* December 26, 1959.
83. *Pravda,* December 23, 1959.
84. *Pravda,* December 27, 1959.
85. *Selskaya Zhizn,* September 18, 1965.
86. *Selskaya Zhizn,* December 2, 1965.
87. Zaslavskaya, pp. 122–4.
88. *Ibid.*
89. *XXIII S'ezd KPSS,* Vol. 1, p. 68.
90. *Ibid.,* p. 136.
91. *Ibid.,* p. 300.
92. *Ibid.,* p. 443.
93. *Ibid.,* Vol. 2, p. 309.

IV

Living and Working
Conditions on the Farms

The detailed, daily supervision and administration of agriculture is the concern of a double set of organs: the government agencies, and the party apparatus. As in all other spheres, the distinction between their functions is often blurred, but it is the latter which plays the decisive rôle.

Ultimate responsibility for party direction of agriculture lies with the General Secretary, Brezhnev, who, like Khrushchev, has personally identified himself with the task of solving the country's agricultural difficulties and has introduced the post-Khrushchev régime's major policy innovations in this sphere. The interlocking of the party and government control apparatus is illustrated in the person of Polyansky, the next most senior official responsible for agriculture, who combines membership of the party Politburo with the post of First Deputy Chairman of the governmental Council of Ministers (there are two First Deputy Chairmen under the Chairman, Kosygin).

The party agricultural apparatus at the General Secretary's disposal is directed by a junior member of the Secretariat, Kulakov. He is head of the CPSU CC's agricultural department, to which are subordinate agricultural departments at each of the lower party levels—in the Republic party Central Committees, and in the *oblast/krai* and *raion* party Committees. The departments' most important function seems to be the selection and appointment of party officials responsible for agriculture. In addition to the party agricultural departments, all provincial party First Secretaries have a primary responsibility for agriculture. The First Secretary of a Republic's Central Committee, of an *obkom*, *kraikom* or *raikom*, ultimately answers for agriculture in his area, and in those districts where

[88]

agriculture is especially important (e.g. the Kuban or the Virgin Lands) his whole career and reputation depend on the results he can achieve in this sector. Another Secretary, in addition to the First Secretary, is usually, at each level, given special responsibilities for agriculture.

Party Committees at each level have their schedule of appointments (*nomenklatura*) for which they are responsible as the appointing or confirming authority. Until early 1954, responsibility for the appointment of *kolkhoz* chairmen lay with the *raikom*. A Central Committee decree of March 2, 1954, however, ordered that such appointments were to be transferred to the *nomenklatura* of the *obkom*, or of a Republic Central Committee (in Republics without *oblast* division), while the *raikom's* responsibility extended only to the posts of deputy chairman, leaders of field brigades and managers of livestock farms.[1]

The hiring and firing of all key officials in a *kolkhoz* are therefore securely in the hands of the local party authorities, though the farm itself ostensibly elects or appoints them.[2] If the *kolkhozniks* attempt to resist the appointment of official nominees, the local authorities may employ various forms of pressure and intimidation to get their way (e.g. deprive the farm of fertiliser, spare parts and building materials, or institute an 'investigation' of the farm by the local procurator).[3] One of the characteristics of the *kolkhoz* system is the frequent and arbitrary replacing of farm officials, especially the chairmen. In 1960, *Pravda* published a letter from a Ukrainian *kolkhoz* which had had twenty different chairmen since the end of the war.[4]

At the base of the pyramid of party controls, below the *raikom*, are the primary party organisations in the farms. These are party Committees in larger farms with over 50 party members or candidates, or party organisations. Both are run by a Secretary and deputy Secretary. The former may be a full-time paid party official if there are more than 150 Communists in the farm. There may also be separate party organisations or groups in the subdivisions of the farm (e.g. in the field brigades or livestock units). The farm's party organisation, or Committee, has the statutory right 'to control the activity of the administration' (Article 60 of the CPSU Statutes).

On the governmental side, the USSR Ministry of Agriculture has direct 'responsibility for the state of agricultural production in the country's collective and State farms'.[5] The Ministry is divided up into a large number of Main Administrations for the different branches of agriculture (e.g. for grain crops, livestock, fodder, soil conservation, etc.) and also has a Main Administration for State Farms and an Administration for Collective Farm Affairs. It has subordinate counterpart Ministries in the Republics (which have Administrations for Collective Farm Affairs and for State Farms) and, below these, Agricultural Administrations in the *krais* and *oblasts* (which have Departments for Collective Farm Affairs and for State Farms), and, finally, Agricultural Production Administrations in the *raions*.[6] Specialised State farms are organised in 'trusts', which are responsible to the *krai* and *oblast* Agricultural Administrations.[7]

The *raion* Agricultural Production Administrations include among their functions 'ensuring the fulfilment of plans for production and State procurements by each *kolkhoz* and *sovkhoz*'.[8] They also 'organise the conclusion of contracts between the *sovkhozes* and *kolkhozes* on the one hand, and the procurement agencies on the other, and control the fulfilment of the contracts'.[9] The principle of dual subordination does not apply to these *raion* Agricultural Administrations. They are not subordinate to the *raion* Soviet's Executive Committees as most other local government agencies are, but only to the next highest rung in the Ministry of Agriculture—the *oblast* or *krai* Agricultural Administrations.[10] Dual subordination does, however, apply above the *raion* level.

The other government agencies directly concerned with agriculture are: *Soyuzselkhoztekhnika* ('The All-Union Association of the USSR Council of Ministers for the sale of agricultural equipment, spares, mineral fertiliser and other technical equipment and for the organisation of the repair and use of machinery on collective and State farms'), which has local branches at each level down to the *raion*[11]; the State Committee for Procurements of the USSR Council of Ministers, which has local offices down to the *oblast/krai* level (in the Republics there are Ministries or State Committees for grain products and the combined fodder industry), and includes among its functions 'control over the maintenance of State discipline in the sale and delivery of agricultural produce by State and collective farms and the procurement organisations'[12]; the USSR Ministry for Land Reclamation and Water Economy, which

[90]

has local offices down to *raion* level and is primarily concerned with irrigation and drainage[13]; and the State Planning Committee of the USSR Council of Ministers (*Gosplan*), one of whose deputy Chairmen is responsible for agricultural planning,[14] and in which there is a special department for agriculture.[15]

Police controls in the countryside operate mainly through the Militia. There is also a network of Militia auxiliaries, known as 'rural executives', recruited among the rural population. It was first established in 1924, and developed during the mass collectivisation period.[16] The rural executives are appointed on a basis of one to every 300 inhabitants in all villages with a rural Soviet, and on that of one executive for all other villages. They are nominated by local Soviets from men of between 18 and 50 and women between 18 and 45—excluding those who have a court record, have undergone banishment or are under arrest—and serve for three months. Refusal to serve is a criminal offence. Their duties are to assist the rural Soviet and Militia in fighting crime, in the protection of State property, in conveying people under arrest to their place of confinement, in supervising sanitary and fire precautions and in carrying out local government and court orders. They are specifically obliged to inform the Militia of all 'crimes and occurrences' in the area.

The Militia control the movements of the rural population through the internal passport system (*see* Section I, p. 26). *Kolkhozniks* are still denied passports and debarred from visiting urban centres, except for short periods with special permission from their local Soviet. They may stay without a passport in areas where the passport system is in force (i.e. all urban and frontier areas) for such purposes as conferences, business, or medical treatment, provided that they register such visits with the Militia and can show a certificate from their village Soviet stating their identity and the object of the visit.[17] Resentment at this permanent evidence of second-class citizenship runs deep.[18] In the post-Khrushchev period there have been isolated suggestions that the *kolkhozniks* should be issued with passports, especially since the existing system was not fully effective in preventing their leaving for the towns.[19] A well-publicised experiment to keep young people on the land found that 'they rejected the customary, but ineffective, methods of social influence. First of all, they rejected administrative measures and the so-called "passport régime" in the *kolkhozes*.'[20] But this régime continues.

Kolkhozniks are not even free to move from one *kolkhoz* to another without the permission of both *kolkhozes*, except when members of different farms are married.[21] This is another cause for resentment, and there have been suggestions that when the Model Statutes are revised they should include a provision for *kolkhozniks* to leave their *kolkhoz*, for example, after giving three months' notice.[22]

STATE AND COLLECTIVE
FARMS: NUMBER AND SIZE

In 1966, there were about 37,000 collective farms with an average of about 417 peasant households, 2,800 hectares of arable land, 1,072 head of cattle, 41 tractors, and 829,000 roubles of fixed assets.[23] There were some 52 million *kolkhozniks*,[24] implying an average membership for each *kolkhoz* of about 1,400 (including *kolkhozniks'* dependants and non-working *kolkhozniks*), and for each peasant household of about 3·4. The number of *kolkhozniks* working on the *kolkhozes* on average throughout the year was 18·4 million,[25] implying an average for each *kolkhoz* of just under 500 workers.

State farms are much larger agricultural units than collective farms, despite the policy of greatly increasing the size of the latter from the late 'forties until recently. In 1966, there were 12,200 State farms with an average of 651 workers, 7,300 hectares of arable land, 2,071 head of cattle, 114 tractors and 2,110,000 roubles of fixed assets.[26]

In 1965, State farms held 57·4 per cent of total agricultural land, and 42·6 per cent of the total sown area. The comparable figures for the collective farms were 41·2 per cent and 50·2 per cent.[27] In the same year, an average of 8 million State farmers and 17·6 million collective farmers worked in agriculture.[28]

VARIATIONS IN CONDITIONS

Conditions on the farms, especially on the *kolkhozes*, vary enormously according to their economic strength, and this does not necessarily depend on whether the farm is well managed or well situated (climatically or geographically), but quite possibly on circumstances such as whether a *kolkhoz* chairman has enjoyed the favour of the local party authorities, or has been adept in securing favourable agricultural delivery tasks. This accounts for the great variation in pay in neighbouring farms. In 1961, in *kolkhozes* in the Gorky *oblast*, pay per work-day was over 22 times higher in the best paying farms than in the worst paying.[29] Large annual variations in pay also occur in *kolkhozes* because of the weather. In areas of insufficient rainfall 'a reduction in average pay in the mass of *kolkhozes* of 25–30 per cent, and even of 50 per cent compared with the previous year, is no exception'.[30]

'Economically weak' collective farms—i.e. farms which year after year operate at a loss; are chronically in debt; cannot expand production, pay their members the minimum rates, or invest in capital equipment—are one of the central problems of Soviet agriculture. A Soviet economist has described 'the exceptionally acute and complicated problem of economically weak *kolkhozes*... [which] cause enormous damage to the national economy as much as to the *kolkhozniks*, whose labour does not receive the appropriate remuneration and whose living standards are declining'.[31] According to another expert, even in Republics with a relatively high average rate of profitability in their farms, many operate at a loss; and 'in 1965, of 36,300 *kolkhozes* in the country, about 10,000, or a quarter of the farms, had incomes... lower than their production expenses'. The level of profitability in a further 10,000 farms was 'clearly unsatisfactory'. In 1966, the number of unprofitable and low-profit farms fell, but there were still about 12,000, or a third, which were in this category. In 1965, about half the State farms were run at a loss, and in 1966 (a very good harvest year) about 25 per cent.[32]

THE COLLECTIVE FARM
(a) INTERNAL ORGANISATION

The organisation of collective farms is laid down in Chapter 8 of the 1935 Model Statutes.[33]

The *kolkhoz* is said to be run by its 'highest organ of administration'—the general meeting of *kolkhozniks*. This statement bears even less relation to reality than does Article 30 of the Soviet Constitution, which says that the USSR Supreme Soviet is 'the highest organ of State power in the USSR'. Apart from anything else, the membership of most *kolkhozes* is far too large for them to hold regular consultations or to act in any sense as administrative organs. In some, there are several thousand members. To have a genuine meeting of them would be a practical impossibility. Various substitutes for general meetings have been devised, such as meetings of *kolkhozniks*' 'representatives',[34] elected by them, or field brigade meetings, but these arrangements seem entirely haphazard. As Brezhnev put it at the March, 1965, plenum: 'In many *kolkhozes*, the bulk of the members are in practice excluded from the discussion and decision of the most important questions.'[35]

It is the *kolkhoz* board, headed by its chairman and supposedly 'elected' by the general meeting—but in reality appointed and dismissed by the local party apparatus (see above)—which in fact runs the farm. The board and chairman are 'elected' for two years. The board should be composed of between five and nine members. It usually includes an agronomist, a veterinary expert, an agricultural engineer and other specialist-technicians. The chairman is required to consult with his board not less than twice a month. The board appoints one of its members as deputy chairman, on the recommendation of the chairman, and also appoints the heads of field brigades and livestock units for not less than two years, plus an accountant.

The farm also has an auditing and checking commission 'elected' by the general meeting.This must not include members of the board or their relatives, or others such as storemen, cashiers, etc., whose work is subject to audit. The commission is supposed to check not only the farm's financial affairs but its adherence to legal norms, and its fulfilment of State obligations and plans. If it discovers anything untoward 'if need be, it informs the investigating organisations'.[36]

Despite all the evidence to the contrary the pretence is usually kept up in official propaganda that the *kolkhozes* are run democratically. For this purpose the concept of '*kolkhoz* democracy', said to be 'the basis for the entire system of administration in *kolkhozes*',[37] has been invented. The official definition of '*kolkhoz* democracy' in a legal handbook[38] begins with the simple assertion: 'The *kolkhozniks* themselves decide all the most important questions in the life of their *kolkhoz*.' That this is untrue—even technically—was admitted not only by Brezhnev at the March, 1965, plenum, but again in October, 1965, in an RSFSR decree which admitted that 'in many cases the *kolkhozniks* are prevented from participating in the decision of important questions relating to the conduct of the farm'.[39]

At the beginning of 1967, a deputy chairman of the Juridical Commission attached to the USSR Council of Ministers confessed:

'The *kolkhoz* Statutes are frequently infringed. Questions involving the acceptance of new members, the expulsion of *kolkhozniks*, confirmation of labour agreements and the acquisition and sale of the basic means of production, are decided by *kolkhoz* managements without subsequent confirmation by general meetings of *kolkhozniks*.'[40]

A decree published at the end of 1967 in Azerbaidjan recorded that not only general meetings, but sessions of the *kolkhoz* board, were rarely held in some of the Republic's farms, and 'many questions are decided unilaterally by the chairman'.[41]

(b) LABOUR ORGANISATION AND DISCIPLINE

Chapter 7 of the Model Statutes establishes the basic principles for organising the work of the *kolkhozniks*. It provides for the formation of 'field brigades' and for the assignment to them of an area of the farm and the equipment necessary for its cultivation for an entire crop-rotation period, and for the allocation of the farm's livestock and equipment to 'livestock brigades' for not less than three years.

The 'brigadier' in charge of a field brigade is not expected to participate in its work. He organises and controls it and keeps a written record of its progress. A 'livestock-brigadier' does, however, participate in the actual work of his brigade.[42] Brigadiers make weekly entries in the work-books of the members of their brigade showing how much work they have done. They may have special accountants to assist them, and in tractor brigades there are assistant brigadiers who are mechanics. 'Links' may be formed, either within the brigades or as independent units, comprising half a dozen or more workers under the command of a 'link-man'. He is appointed either by the *kolkhoz* board or by a meeting of the brigade of which the link is a part.[43]

All work must be carried out in accordance with 'internal regulations' approved by the farm's general meeting. These

[95]

regulations are 'considerably wider in their scope' than the analogous 'rules of internal labour order' in industrial enterprises, because they 'govern not merely the farm's economic and production activity, but also some aspects of the life of *kolkhozniks* and *kolkhoz* households'.[44] In particular, they fix the farm's working hours, days off and holidays; the minimum number of annual and seasonal work-days, or norms, a *kolkhoznik* must fulfil, and the minimum times he must turn out for work (the brigadier renders to the board a daily return of *kolkhozniks* who fail to appear or appear late at work)[45]; punishments (the heaviest of which is expulsion from the *kolkhoz*) and rewards; a list of the misdemeanours constituting infringement of labour discipline; and the conditions under which the 'personal requirements' of a *kolkhoznik* may be met—for example, the conditions under which he may have the use of a *kolkhoz* horse or transport (this normally depends on his having fulfilled the minimum required work on the farm, and must be paid for).

Each farm establishes the minimum amount of work which all ordinary *kolkhozniks* (except children under 16, the disabled, men over 60 and women over 55) must do on the farm. This may be in terms of minimum labour-days earned, norms fulfilled, or 'appearances at work'. Not only are annual minima set, but also seasonal and monthly. The minima are also differentiated according to the age, sex and other characteristics of the *kolkhozniks*. Thus, a farm in the Perm *oblast* set minimum monthly norms for 'able-bodied *kolkhozniks*', 'women without children', and 'women with pre-schoolchildren and schoolchildren'. They were highest in July–September (25 norms a month for the able-bodied), and lowest in October–March (20 norms a month).[46] Not surprisingly, there is pressure for the abolition of work minima, and this has been proposed in connexion with suggestions for revising the Model Statutes.[47]

Even if a *kolkhoznik* has fulfilled his minimum for a given period, this does not mean he has no further obligation to work on the farm in that period.[48] *Kolkhozniks* are expected to work longer on the farm, during the year as a whole, than workers in the factory: for statistical purposes they are considered to have been fully employed throughout the year only if they completed 290 man-days (270 in the case of women), whereas industrial workers average only 266·5 man-days per year.[49]

In addition to fulfilling their obligations to work on the farm, *kolkhozniks* must perform an annual *corvée*. A decree of April 7, 1950,[50] provided that State and collective farms must participate in the building and maintenance of local roads at their own expense. Each *kolkhoz* must carry out road-work on the basis of four to six days' work per able-bodied *kolkhoznik* per year, and two to four days' work per item of *kolkhoz* machinery (including tractors and trucks) and draught power suitable for roadwork. Instead of performing this *corvée*, farms may, 'in exceptional circumstances', be permitted by local Soviets to make an equivalent monetary payment.

Punishments are not supposed to be imposed by farm officials without the board's approval, and expulsion requires the sanction of a general meeting (an open, majority vote, with at least two-thirds of the members attending).[51] The penalty for not fulfilling the required amount of work on the farm may be one or more of the following: a tax increase of 50 per cent; exclusion from the right to receive fodder from the farm, or use its pastures, for private livestock; a reduction in size of the private plot. Other punishments are: the repeating of work which has been poorly done; a reprimand before a general meeting; the forfeiting of labour-day units; inclusion on 'the board of shame' (a public notice board devoted to portraits of miscreants with short accounts of their misdemeanours); and transfer to lower-paid work.[52]

For 'educational' purposes, offenders may sometimes be brought before the farm's 'comrades' court', elected from the *kolkhoz* membership, public sessions of which are the occasion for dramatising before a large audience the perils of 'anti-social behaviour'.

The pressure to discipline the farms has given rise to a special *corpus* of 'agricultural crimes', unique to the Soviet system. For example, any attempt by a *kolkhoznik* to expand his private plot at the expense of *kolkhoz* land, or beyond the statutory limits, consitutes a criminal act under a decree of May 27, 1939. It is normally punishable under Article 199 of the RSFSR Criminal Code, which provides for penalties of up to a year's corrective labour.[53] Under Article 168 of the Code, wilful damage to *kolkhoz* or *sovkhoz* crops can be punished by up to a year's corrective labour. Under Khrushchev, the Code was extended to provide that 'criminal negligence' in using or maintaining farm machinery be punished by up to three years' deprivation of freedom.[54]

The length of the working day varies from farm to farm. The average is about eight hours, but in some farms, particularly those in which the earnings are low and discipline is weak, it may be only five-and-a-half to six hours. In some stronger farms it may be as much as ten hours.[55] Normally, longer hours are worked on animal husbandry than on field-work. Individual *kolkhozniks*, particularly women, occasionally work appallingly long hours. At the March, 1965, plenum, Pavlov (the Komsomol leader) remarked: 'It is considered normal for a milkmaid to be on the livestock farm for between 12 and 14 hours a day, and to go without a day off for years on end.' He told of one, aged about 30, who had not had a day off for 15 years.[56] A story published in 1964 quoted a milkmaid as saying that on her farm, where they 'rise at dawn, go to bed at midnight and catch up with their sleep in snatches by day', there were

'no days off, no holidays; it's as if we're fettered, there isn't even time to go to town and buy oneself something'.[57]

Kolkhoz chairmen, brigadiers and other officials can insist on *kolkhozniks* working overtime, starting work earlier than usual, and working at night.[58]

Sunday is the normal day off, but in some farms there is a rota system for taking a day off. The *kolkhoz* board may declare a public holiday to be a working day. Some economically strong farms give their *kolkhozniks* annual paid holidays (normally 12 working days a year), but only to those who have fulfilled the required minimum amount of work on the farm.[59]

The five-day working week, which has recently been introduced in industry, is only practised in 'certain progressive State and collective farms'.[60]

There is considerable seasonal unemployment during the winter and, according to Polyansky, 'many rural inhabitants are employed in communal production for several months only'.[61] Soviet estimates showed that 25 million *kolkhozniks* were at work on the farms in July, 1962, but only 14·5 million in January.[62] To help provide winter employment, a decree of September 16, 1967, encouraged farms to establish their own 'auxiliary enterprises' for processing agricultural produce and for making building materials, consumer goods and other articles from local raw materials and industrial waste.[63] The danger is that these auxiliary enterprises may distract the peasants from their work on the farms, but the authorities are alive to this, and to the need 'to prevent the infiltration into the auxiliary enterprises of so-called "*shabashniks*" [illegal private operators] who try to use them for extracting unearned income'.[64]

(d) WAGES

Until recently, the usual method of paying *kolkhozniks* was the 'labour-day' system (*see* Section I, pp. 36–7). The defects of this system have long been apparent, and were well summarised by a Soviet economist as follows:

'Kolkhozniks are paid long after their work, and their pay remains quantitatively undetermined for a lengthy period. For many months the *kolkhoznik* knows how many labour-days he has earned but has only the vaguest idea of how much he will receive for them. Annual fluctuations in payment per labour-day adversely affect the *kolkhozniks'* material interests, and increase the stimulus for them to give prior attention to their private plots. The size of the fund for labour payments, under this system of income distribution, does not depend on the number of labour-days. It is not established as an independent quantity, as part of the *kolkhoz's* production expenses, but passively, as the residue of monetary income and produce after production expenses have been met, obligations to the State fulfilled, and communal funds replenished.'[65]

Since 1958, most of the farms have combined the labour-day system with monthly or quarterly advances of cash and produce, and a few began to discard the labour-day system altogether in favour of the monetary accounting and payment of labour, based on various rates for the fulfilment of work-norms. By 1965, 30,000 *kolkhozes* were still on the labour-day system, and some 8–0,000 were on a monetary system which, however, still retained a large element—about 10 per cent—of payment in kind. Only a few farms paid only in money.[66] The slow progress in the monetisation of payments was caused by insufficient funds, especially in economically weak farms, by the fact that (until 1966) the farms' income tax was based on their distributions in money, but not in kind,[67] and by the *kolkhozniks'* requirements for agricultural produce, both for their own needs and for marketing at favourable prices.

Speakers at the March, 1965, plenum emphasised the low level of pay in *kolkhozes* compared with that in *sovkhozes* and, even more, with that in industry. In the Pskov *oblast*, for example, it averaged about half that in the *sovkhozes*, and only a third that in industry.[68]

At the 23rd Party Congress in March, 1966, Brezhnev announced a proposal to introduce gradually, over the following five years, guaranteed monthly payments for *kolkhozniks*, based on *sovkhoz* rates and labour-norms.[69] A decree of May 16, 1966, 'recommended' that a start be made from July 1, 1966. The guaranteed pay would be in both cash and kind, and *kolkhozes* with insufficient funds would get five-year loans from the State Bank.[70] By the beginning of 1967, it was claimed that about 90 per cent of the farms had begun introducing this system.[71] Almost 75 per cent have also now abandoned the labour-day in favour of a monetary system of payment (in which, however, there remains an element of payment in produce—15 per cent in 1966).[72] It seems to be common practice to withhold 20 per cent to 30 per cent of the monetary payment due to the *kolkhozniks* until the end of the year, when the amount of produce available for distribution can be ascertained. This produce is then priced so as to make it total the withheld monetary payment, and is distributed accordingly, under the guise of 'the sales of produce to *kolkhozniks*'.[73]

Before the May, 1966, decree on the adoption in *kolkhozes* of a payment system modelled on that of the *sovkhozes*, many farms had experimented with the idea, but it had been criticised by reformist economists on two grounds:

(a) Weak *kolkhozes* had insufficient funds to maintain such a system, and 'this merely led to over-expenditure of funds, to great indebtedness, to the exhaustion of reserve funds built up earlier for regular [pay] advances, and finally to a sharp decline in payment rates for labour in subsequent years. Life clearly confirms that the *kolkhozes*' tariff system must be built on the basis of the actual level of their incomes.'[74]

(b) *Kolkhozes* require a much more highly differentiated system than that operating in *sovkhozes* because they are more concerned than are *sovkhozes* (which rely on 'administrative orders' and 'State discipline') with providing complex incentives for the performance of different tasks.[75]

The *sovkhoz* pay system (consisting of 12 six-grade scales, giving a total of 72 different pay rates) is itself admitted to be 'complicated and imperfect'.[76] The conversion to it of *kolkhozes* seems to have produced even greater complexity. In the Ukraine, for example, the Ministry of Agriculture has approved over 160 pay rates, based on 28 different (six-grade) scales, 'with various coefficients and assessments which are uncoordinated'.[77]

It is also clear that many *kolkhozes* are still unable to find the necessary funds to bring their payments in line with *sovkhoz* rates (confirming what the critics said earlier). Polyansky, at the end of 1967, blamed difficulties in introducing the new system on the State Bank: 'Certain officials of the State Bank have several times tried to "put a spoke in the wheels" of its introduction, and halted the issue of credits for guaranteed pay'.[78] *Izvestiya* also claimed that these officials had adopted the attitude that 'profitable farms are not supposed to have credits, and unprofitable ones cannot be given them'. Bank officials, it revealed, were naturally loath to sanction credits to economically weak farms, because their bonuses depended on securing the repayment of credits.[79] Some idea of wage rates and of the wage structure in *kolkhozes* under the new system is given by the 'Recommendations on the payment of labour in *kolkhozes*', approved by the RSFSR Council of Ministers on July 2, 1966.[80]

The recommended daily rates for ordinary labourers range from 1·56 roubles to 3·10 roubles, while those for tractor drivers and machine operators range from 2·20 roubles to 6·50 roubles. *Kolkhozniks* work an average of about 200 days[81] a year on the *kolkhoz*, and so these daily rates would mean that an average *kolkhoznik* labourer could receive from his *kolkhoz* between 26 roubles and 51·5 roubles a month, while tractor drivers and machine operators could receive between 36·5 roubles and 108 roubles.

Next come recommended monthly wages for the administrative staff. They range from 40 roubles for guards to 70 to 90 roubles for senior book-keepers. Brigadiers should get a monthly wage ranging between 75 roubles and 180 roubles, according to the value of the production of their brigade. But in special cases they may receive 190 roubles. Chief agronomists, engineers and vets should get between 130 roubles and 250 roubles.

Finally, *kolkhoz* chairmen are divided into 10 categories, according to the economic importance of their *kolkhoz*, judged primarily by its income over the previous three to five years, and are recommended to receive between 140 roubles and 300 roubles a month, though in exceptional cases they may get a maximum of 330 roubles.

All members of a *kolkhoz* may earn additional pay on top of their basic wages, according to the results of their work (e.g. by overfulfilling plans and work-norms). In the case of *kolkhoz* chairmen and senior specialists, this may amount to as much as an additional six months' wages in one year. In 1966, the additional pay of *kolkhozniks* as a whole is said to have equalled 10 per cent of their basic wages.[82]

The great difference in basic pay between *kolkhoz* chairmen and their senior officials on the one hand, and labourers on the other—the differential could be greater than 10:1—is a striking feature of this wage structure. It is no doubt even greater if additional pay is taken into account.

Another feature is the very low remuneration of the bulk of *kolkhozniks*—the ordinary labourers. The grave consequences of this for the nation as a whole have been spelt out by a reformist economist:

> The main producer of agricultural output is the *kolkhoz* sector—about two-thirds of the country's output comes from it. The low level of pay and the *kolkhozniks'* feeble material incentives to work are one of the main factors behind the slow development of agriculture . . . The growing demand for food while the volume of its production remained constant led to interruptions in food supplies to the population, to purchases of food abroad, and to a retarded growth of the population's living standards. Another consequence of the feeble material incentives of agricultural workers in the results of their labour is the extremely low return on capital investments in agriculture.'[83]

THE STATE FARM
(a) HISTORY

The large, State-operated farm was envisaged at the outset of the Soviet régime as the ideal type of agricultural enterprise which could serve as a model for other farms.

Under the Land Decree of November 8, 1917, highly cultivated land formerly belonging to large landowners, and specially valuable plantations, stud-farms, etc., were not distributed among the peasants but reserved for the State.[84] The 'Law of Socialist Land Tenure and Measures for Transition to Socialist

Agriculture', of February 14, 1919, stated: 'State Farms are being organised (a) to obtain the greatest possible increase in food supplies by raising the productivity of agriculture and extending the crop area; (b) to create conditions for the complete transition to Communist agriculture; and (c) to create and develop centres of best farming techniques'.[85] A Decree of the following day, 'On the Organisation of State Farms by Institutions and Amalgamations of the Industrial Proletariat', provided for the establishment of State farms attached to various factories to produce food for the worker.[86] Thus from the outset, the party relied on urban workers to run the State farms.

In the event, only a very small part of confiscated land was converted into State farms, and by 1921 they covered only 3·3 million hectares.[87] It has been estimated that the joint holdings of collective and State farms at this time accounted for less than four per cent of total agricultural land.[88]

The first, abortive attempt to make the State farms a large-scale success occurred in April, 1928. The Politburo, in an endeavour to solve the procurements crisis, launched a four- to five-year programme for bringing unused land into cultivation under newly established State farms, which were to become 'grain factories' producing an annual marketable supply of 100 million poods (62 poods = 1 ton) of grain.[89] A similar programme for establishing livestock State farms was launched by the 16th Party Congress in 1930.[90]

Between 1929 and 1933, the percentage of the total grain area accounted for by State farms rose from 1·5 to 10·8.[91] But hopes placed in them were not fulfilled. In 1933, grain deliveries were only a third of those planned, while deliveries of sugar beet, cotton and meat amounted to little more than one-tenth of the planned target. The increase in head of livestock was only 50 per cent of what had been hoped.[92]

Stalin told the 17th Party Congress in 1934:

'As for the State farms, it must be said that they still fail to cope with their tasks. I do not in the least underestimate the great revolutionising rôle of our State farms. But if we compare the enormous sums the State has invested in the State farms with the actual results they have achieved to date, we find an enormous discrepancy to the disadvantage of the State farms. The principal reason for the discrepancy is the fact that our State grain farms are too unwieldy; the directors cannot manage such huge farms. The State

[103]

farms themselves are too specialised, they have no crop-rotation or fallow land; they do not include sectors for livestock farming. Evidently, it will be necessary to split up the farms and do away with their excessive specialisation.'[93]

The original stress on concentration and specialisation was thus reversed, 'gigantomania' was denounced, and the farms were reduced in size. They also declined in number—from 4,742 in 1933 to 3,961 in 1938, in which year they accounted for 9·1 per cent of the total sown area and 7·3 per cent of the cattle, and had 1½ million employees.[94]

Under Khrushchev, the number of State farms more than doubled, and at the time of his fall in 1964 there were 10,078.[95] He favoured them as a means of furthering the urbanisation of rural life, and gave them pride of place in his Virgin Lands scheme, under which 425 were set up.[96] In some areas two, three or even four State farms were grouped together to form what was in effect an 'agrotown' with an initial population of up to 4,000.[97] 'In the national interest' much collective farmland was transferred to the *sovkhozes*.[98] At the September, 1953, plenum it was also decided to develop State farms in the immediate vicinity of large towns to supply the urban populations with vegetables and dairy produce.[99] By 1956, the number of State farms specialising in these fields had already reached 340.[100]

Under Khrushchev, the superiority of State farms over collective farms was emphasised in an ideological context. The 1961 Party Programme, for instance, while foreseeing the eventual 'merging of *kolkhoz* property and the property of the whole people into one communal property', defined State farms as 'the leading Socialist agricultural enterprises'. They would 'play an ever-increasing rôle', and 'serve the *kolkhozes* as a model of progressive, scientifically managed, economically profitable social production, of high efficiency and labour productivity'.[101] This emphasis has been dropped by the post-Khrushchev régime, and Brezhnev told the March, 1965, plenum: 'One must suppose that both these types of communal farming will exist and develop for a long time yet.'[102] (*See* Section III, p. 77.)

(*b*) INTERNAL ORGANISATION

The State farm is headed by a director, acting on the basis of 'one-man-management' (*edinonachalie*). His is the ultimate responsibility for all work on the State farm and for fulfilment of plans. He has the right to hire and dismiss workers, apart from senior officials such as the deputy director, chief agronomist and chief accountant, who are on the schedule of appointments (*nomenklatura*) of higher organs of the Ministry of Agriculture.[103] The director is in charge of the farm's finances, receives credits from Gosbank and concludes agreements.[104] In pilot *sovkhozes* set up in 1966, and probably in the 300 transferred to self-accounting in 1967, there is a 'Council' presided over by the director and consisting of senior officials. At least half its members are elected annually by the farm workers.[105] The farms also have their own party and trade union organisations.

Unlike the collective farm, and due to its greater size, the State farm is usually split up into three or more 'sections' or livestock farms (*fermy*) on a territorial basis—a section generally comprising a village or group of villages. The main section will include the central settlement where the administrative offices, repair workshops, main services, schools, clubs and most of the dwelling houses are situated. However, the other sections or *fermy* have their own workshops, storehouses, farm buildings and houses. The sections are divided into brigades and links of various types, corresponding in size and function with those in collective farms. In general, the brigade is assigned permanent personnel, machinery and equipment, livestock and buildings and receives its separate production task for the year.[106]

The administrative superstructure in State farms is considerably greater than in collective farms, chiefly because they are larger. The State farm has an additional category of 'chief specialists' and also heads of section. They are also more fully provided with administrative and specialist staff at lower levels. Administrative and technical staffs (not including tractor drivers) amount to between six and seven per cent of total State farm personnel.[107] Farms also have numerous ancillary brigades for construction, transport, maintenance of electrical equipment, road-building, brick-making, in addition to blacksmiths' shops, educational and medical services, and canteens, for all of which the director is ultimately responsible.

(c) WAGES

The State farm is both owned and managed by the State, and
its employees have much the same conditions of work and
benefits as State employees in non-agricultural sectors. They
are able to join a trade union and can thus participate in the
State social security schemes which are administered by the
unions. As with industrial workers, they are paid according
to rules laid down by the central government. They now receive a guaranteed minimum wage of 60 roubles a month, as
do urban workers.[108] Daily pay scales are laid down for various
types of workers, based on fulfilment of a daily norm. Over-
fulfilment of work-norms can be rewarded with various supplements and bonuses, though these do not appear in practice
to make up a very substantial part of earnings. As in the case
of urban workers, pay is based on a 41-hour, five-day week.
Overtime is permitted, and leave in lieu is granted for it.
Exceptionally, an annual payment may be made for overtime.[109]

There are two main pay scales, one for tractor-driver-
mechanics, the other for ordinary labourers and livestock
workers. They are divided into six grades, and a worker's grade
is determined by his experience and qualifications. The scales
for mechanised workers are split into three groups on a territorial basis.[110] On the other hand, scales for ordinary labourers
are, in principle, standard for all State farms in the Soviet
Union.[111] Scales for piece-workers are about 10 per cent higher
than for time-workers to 'compensate for greater intensity of
work.'[112] In any case, the average wage works out the same.[113]
Most workers in both State and collective farms are, in fact,
piece-workers.

Several types of bonus are payable in addition to basic rates,
although the type and extent depend on the branch of agriculture and the type of farming (for instance the degree of
mechanisation and the type of crop). Extra awards are sometimes paid to workers on various priority crops. This supplementary pay may not exceed one-and-a-half months' basic pay
in a year. The scales according to which daily rates of payment
are made are shown in the following table.[114]

Bonuses (*premia*) are paid for overfulfilment of farms' production plans. Bonuses are usually paid out to the brigade,
detachment or link responsible for the particular crop, although
some bonuses can be paid to individuals, especially in live-

[106]

Daily Rates of Pay for State Farm Workers
(Roubles and kopecks)

	Grades					
	I	II	III	IV	V	VI
	R. k.	R. k.	R. k.	R. k.	R. k.	R. k.
1. Manual and Live-stock Work						
Time-workers	1–56·3	1–73·5	1–95·4	2–20·4	2–48·5	2–81·3
Piece-workers	1–72·0	1–90·8	2–15·0	2–42·4	2–73·3	3–09·6
2. Tractor drivers and Mechanics:						
Time-workers						
1st Group	2–20	2–50	2–90	3–20	3–80	4–50
2nd Group	2–60	3–00	3–50	3–90	4–50	5–40
3rd Group	2–80	3–30	3–80	4–20	4–90	5–90
Piece-workers	2–40	2–80	3–20	3–60	4–20	5–00
2nd Group	2–90	3–40	3–80	4–30	5–00	6–00
3rd Group	3–10	3–60	4–20	4–70	5–50	6–50

stock farming. How much is paid for a given degree of over-fulfilment again depends on the type of agriculture and the crop, but in any case such *premia* must not exceed 40 per cent of piece-rate earnings for the year.[115] Time-workers are not eligible for such bonuses, but may receive an addition of up to 20 per cent of their basic scale during the year.[116]

Supervisory staff, such as the men and women in charge of the brigade detachments and links, are paid up to 25 per cent above their rate on the basic scale and also receive bonuses. Their position on the scale is usually between grades three and six.[117]

The payment system has been described as 'very complicated' and 'hard for workers to understand'.[118] There was considerable criticism of the payment of labour in State farms at the March, 1965, plenum of the CPSU CC. One speaker said the system was 'so imperfect that it puts a brake on production', and that 'highly productive work is paid even worse than work of medium or low productivity.'[119] Since this plenum, there have been a few slight amendments to State farm workers' pay structure. Under a party and government decree of April 22, 1966, tractor-driver-mechanics receive long-service supplements, additional harvest pay and better wage terms in off-periods.[120]

Managerial staff—including specialist workers—were until recently guaranteed only 70 per cent of their basic salaries, the other 30 per cent being paid at the end of the year if the output plan was fulfilled.[121] This unpopular system was ended by a decree of April 1, 1965, under which basic salaries are paid in full each month. Staff workers now also receive a supplement of 0·3 per cent of annual salary for every one per cent overfulfilment of the sales or production plan. In addition, they receive a bonus of up to 10 per cent of basic salary for every one per cent over-fulfilment of the same plan. Up to five per cent of the farm's above-plan profit can be distributed among staff workers.[122] The basic salary of a staff worker may be raised or reduced by 10 per cent depending on his education, length of service and qualifications.[123]

The decree of April 1, 1965, also slightly amended the salary scales of staff workers. There is now a ten-point instead of a seven-point scale, and higher-echelon staff workers receive considerably more than hitherto.[124] The intention appears to be to recruit and retain better qualified staff. The larger the enterprise and its output, the higher the salary scale of staff workers. Salary scales of lower-paid staff remain as before. Lower-grade staff, as lower-grade manual workers, are paid at a uniform rate in all State farms throughout the country.[125] The present scales for State farm staff workers are shown in the table on the opposite page.[126]

(d) ECONOMIC ACCOUNTING (KHOZRASCHET)

Throughout their development, an unsuccessful struggle has been waged to make the State farms pay for themselves, initially by putting them on a self-accounting basis. Steps in this direction were taken as early as the end of the civil war: 'At first, State farms were on the State budget. At the end of 1921, they were put on economic accounting.'[127] In fact, they have at all times only been kept solvent by State subsidies. Khrushchev said at the January, 1955, party plenum:

'With proper management no enterprise, let alone a State farm, should be unprofitable. Such a farm has no right to exist'.[128]

Khrushchev was echoed a decade later by Brezhnev, who said at the March, 1965, party plenum:

'The principles of economic accounting have been violated . . . We must renounce excessive regimentation in the distribution of capital investments and subsidies for *sovkhozes* and transfer *sovkhozes* in the near future to full economic accounting.'[129]

Post	Grades									
	I	II	III	IV	V	VI	VII	VIII	IX	X
Director	270–300	250–270	210–250	200	190	180	170	160	150	140
Head agronomist, engineer, zoo technician or veterinary surgeon	230–250	200–230	180–200	170	160	150	140	130	—	—
Head economist	230–250	200–230	180–200	170	—	—	—	—	—	—
Acting head specialists, senior agronomists, engineers, etc.	160–180	160–180	160–180	150–140	150–140	130	120	120	120	120
Head of work-shop, senior agronomist, etc.	120–140	120–140	120–140	120	120	110	110	110	100	100
Head, or acting head, accountant	170–180	160–170	150–160	140	130	120	120	110	100	100
Agronomists, zoo technicians, veterinary surgeons, economists, engineers, etc.	110–120	110–120	110–120	110	110	100	100	100	95	95
Senior technician	70–80	70–80	70–80	70–80	70–80	70–80	70–80	70–80	70–80	70–80
Technicians of all types	60–70	60–70	60–70	60–70	60–70	60–70	60–70	60–70	60–70	60–70

Despite all efforts, the *sovkhozes* have only paid their way on a nationwide basis on two occasions since their inception in 1919. In 1956, they are said to have 'made a profit for the first time, though a considerable number still ran at a loss'.[130] And they again finished the financial year with a profit, 'for the first time for a number of years', in 1966.[131] These were outstanding crop years in districts where State farms predominate. More recently, in 1963, almost 70 per cent operated at a loss and required State subsidies of nearly three milliard roubles.[132]

[109]

In 1934, a year of bumper harvests, the *sovkhozes* made an overall loss of 764 million roubles[133] and 62 per cent were unprofitable.[134] In 1965, this figure had dropped to 48 per cent, but only as a result of raised prices.[135]

This poor performance can be ascribed to a number of factors, principally managerial incompetence, unrealistic prices, and the feather-bedding effect of State subsidies.

Under the post-Khrushchev régime, the State farms have been helped by the increased delivery prices introduced in 1965, which raised their incomes in that year by an estimated two milliard roubles, and by an earlier decision that a *sovkhoz* would be permitted to retain 42 per cent of profit obtained.[136] A pilot scheme for running State farms on an economic accounting basis was announced late in 1965.[137] They were to receive the same procurement prices as the local *kolkhozes*, i.e., about 10 per cent more.

The next step was the announcement on April 15, 1967, that 390 State farms (about three per cent of the total) were to be put immediately on full economic accounting, including all State farms in the Estonian Republic and Voronezh *oblast*.[138] In the event, 406 were transferred.[139] In these farms, 15 per cent of planned profit was to go to the material incentive fund, 10 per cent for social and cultural construction and housing, 20 per cent to a controlled insurance fund (in the previous year, 70–80 per cent coverage of crop value had been urged)[140] and 10 per cent to capital investment. Since the remaining profit (i.e. 45 per cent) was to go to centralised funds for investment etc., it appears that richer State farms are expected to foot the bills of the poorer, despite objections.[141]

AGRICULTURAL PROCUREMENTS
AND THE CONTRACT SYSTEM

The farms' obligations to fulfil their deliveries of produce to the State dominate all their activity. The State continues to enforce the fulfilment of obligations ruthlessly and without regard for peasant interests. A Soviet economist has commented:

'The small effect of material incentives in *kolkhoz* production at the present stage stems from the existence of a deep contradiction between society's interests and those of the *kolkhozes*, concerning a central point of their economic relations: the State procurements of *kolkhoz* produce. The State procurements, which are extremely necessary for satisfying the requirements of the national economy, are still often disadvantageous for the *kolkhozes*, and are carried out in many cases against their material interests and with the aid of administrative measures.'[142]

The procurement system is based on annual and long-term procurement plans for each of the main agricultural products throughout the country, broken down according to Republics. They are drawn up by the USSR Ministry of Agriculture and approved by the USSR Council of Ministers. The USSR Council of Ministers also approves procurement prices for the different products and their differential rates according to Republics. Republic Councils of Ministers are responsible for procurement plans only for minor crops such as vegetables, fruits and honey, destined for local consumption, and even these must be communicated to the USSR *Gosplan* and to the Central Statistical Office. The procurement plans are passed down from the USSR Council of Ministers to the Republic Council of Ministers, to the *krai/oblast* Soviet Executive Committees, to the *raion* Agricultural Production Administrations which, finally, use them 'as the basis for distributing procurement tasks among individual collective and State farms'.[143]

How the *raion* administrations carry this out is left vague. They are supposed to adopt 'a differentiated approach to each farm, taking into consideration the long-term development of its economy, specialisation, and the need to leave produce in the farm for expanding production (seed and fodder), and for the personal needs of the *kolkhozniks*.'[144] But 'the question of how, in fact, to distribute the procurement plan among the farms has not been decided', and local authorities have been left to work out their own methods, 'many of which have no scientific basis'[145]. The commonest of these methods seems to be to fix the plan for each farm on the basis of its 'achieved level' in previous years.

Although deliveries of produce surplus to the plan are supposedly voluntary, they also are planned:

'The volumes of free deliveries of agricultural produce are annually determined by the USSR *Gosplan* with the USSR Ministry of Agriculture and submitted for approval to the USSR Council of Ministers. They are established by taking into account harvest prospects for the crops to be delivered, and are distributed to each Union Republic. Plans for free deliveries are given to the procurement agencies. They are not given to collective and State farms.'[146]

In practice, the 'free deliveries' of staple produce are regarded as just as compulsory as the basic, planned deliveries:

'In connexion with the exceptionally tight situation with regard to the country's grain balance, the principle that the *kolkhozes* may freely dispose of their surplus-to-plan produce will not find its full expression for several years to come. Together with the basic fixed plan for grain sales by Republics, *krais* and *oblasts*, a compulsory plan is also set for additional sales. The result is a system of "two plans", the difference being that under the first produce is sold at the basic procurement price, and under the second it is sold at one-and-a-half times the price.'[147]

The farms' planned deliveries are the basis for annual contracts which they must conclude, under the supervision of the *raion* agricultural administrations, with the procurement agencies. The main agencies are the Ministries of Grain Products, Food, Meat and Milk, Light Industry, Trade, Agriculture and Health, and the Consumer Co-operatives. The multiplicity of agencies admittedly causes confusion.[148]

Contracts are supposed to be concluded by not later than January 1 each year, but this is rarely achieved.[149] Separate contracts are concluded for each product to be delivered.[150] The contracts are supposed to be concluded on the farms, and the representatives of the procurement agencies are supposed to visit the farms for this purpose. (In practice. there are cases in which representatives 'demanded that the leaders of the collective and State farms themselves should appear at the reception points, at enterprises or in *raion* centres, or sent the farms draft contracts by post'.)[151] Above-plan deliveries are specified either in the basic contracts or in separate ones.[152]

The contracts specify the quantities and types of produce to be delivered and sold, as previously determined by the plan. They also specify delivery dates and places, and the procurement agency's responsibilities for accepting and paying for the produce. Finally, they provide for penalties (fines) for non-fulfilment of obligations by either side.[153]

In reality, the contracts have little force, and are often empty formalities: 'Unfortunately a formal attitude is often adopted towards the contract agreements, and the sanctions and material responsibility for which they provide are not applied.'[154] Certainly they offer small protection to the farms in their dealings with the procurement agencies:

'The agreements between the *kolkhozes* and the procurement

organisations often do not meet legal requirements, and are concluded without taking the *kolkhozes'* interests into account. In many cases, as a result of the infringement of planning, contractual and financial discipline, the rights and interest of agricultural workers are damaged.'[155]

In August, 1966, despite the contracts, more than 1½ million head of fattened pigs, which collective and State farms in the RSFSR were to deliver, were not accepted by the procurement agencies at the proper time, because the processing industry had refused them. In the Ukraine, in the first half of 1966, more than 306,000 head of cattle and 560,000 pigs were not accepted from the farms. In the RSFSR, in some years, up to 30 per cent of vegetables for delivery are not accepted by the procurement agencies, even though urban centres are short of supplies.[156]

Since the contracts have so little practical significance, and the deliveries of produce for which they provide have already been assigned to the farms as 'planned tasks', one may wonder what their purpose is. The answer seems to be that they are necessary not so much to regulate the procurement process as to provide a democratic façade for it:

'What is the practical significance of establishing contractual relations in agricultural procurements and, above all, in the process of fulfilling the planned centralised procurements of *kolkhoz* and *sovkhoz* produce . . . ? Contractual relations best of all comply with the principle of democratic centralism. . . . This form corresponds more fully with the character of the *kolkhozes*, whose expression of their intent, as owners of the produce, is the necessary condition for its disposal also under the firm procurement plans.'[157]

Superimposed on the plan and contracts for procurements is the vast propaganda campaign, perpetually put out by the party and its 'agriprop' apparatus, for over-fulfilment of targets and the assumption of new 'undertakings', in 'Socialist competition'. The first secretary of the Nikolaev *oblast* party committee reported recently, for example, that collective farmers in his *oblast* 'on the initiative of the party organisation, have reconsidered the obligations adopted earlier and have undertaken to increase the harvest of all grains this year to 25 centners a hectare, and of winter wheat to 30 centners. They are striving to fulfil the Five-Year Plan for the sale of grain to the State in three years . . . Many other farms in the *oblast* have started a campaign to fulfil the Five-Year-Plan for grain sales to the State in four years. The remaining collective and State farms are trying to follow their example.'[158]

PRIVATE PLOTS

As has been shown in the earlier sections of this study (Section I, pp. 33–5; Section II, pp. 54, 58, 65–6; Section III, pp. 73–4), the authorities have, ever since collectivisation, blown hot and cold on these vestiges of traditional peasant farming to suit the needs of the moment. At present, they are pursuing a line of guarded encouragement. Polyansky recently re-emphasised the view that although the plots would eventually disappear, this would not happen 'soon or all at once', and that they had meanwhile a useful function to perform, not only for the peasants but for the economy as a whole.[159]

Official figures show how indispensable the plots in fact are. In 1966, they produced 63 per cent of the country's potatoes, 41 per cent of vegetables, 54 per cent of fruit and berries, 40 per cent of meat, 39 per cent of milk, 67 per cent of eggs and 20 per cent of wool. From this source (which includes the private plots of State farm workers and urban workers) came 44 per cent of the marketed potatoes, 37 per cent of the eggs, 17 per cent of the meat, 14 per cent of the wool, 12 per cent of the vegetables and seven per cent of the milk.[160] Although the plots only occupy about three per cent of the total sown area, they appear to be responsible for about a third of total agricultural production, and for as much as 40 per cent of livestock production.[161] The plots usually average less than a third of a hectare, but there appear to be as many as 50 million of them.

Most of the produce of the plots is not marketed but consumed by the peasants (in the RSFSR, 70 per cent of the milk, 66 per cent of the meat and 90 per cent of the potatoes produced on the plots is estimated to be consumed by the plot-holders). Between 75 per cent and 100 per cent of the potatoes, vegetables, milk, meat and eggs consumed by *kolkhozniks* comes from their plots.[162]

The plots give the *kolkhozniks* a much bigger return for their labour than the collective farm. In 1963–5, they spent 60 per cent of their working time, on average, on the farm, obtaining from this source only 37 per cent of their income; and

30 per cent of their working time on the plots, from which they obtained over 35 per cent of their income.[163]

Work on the plots is largely the task of women. In the RSFSR, male able-bodied *kolkhozniks* spent on average only nine per cent of their working time on the plots; women over 33 per cent.[164]

Though the post-Khrushchev régime has indicated an intention of tolerating and modestly supporting private plots, there is much uncertainty (as always) about how far toleration and support can or should go. Confusion over the issue began with the lifting of the Khrushchev restrictions at the end of 1964. When they were lifted, 'no kind of new concrete recommendations were issued about the possible sizes of private plots and the number of private cattle ... It was merely stated that the norms in force before the introduction of the unjustified limitations should be restored. But which norms? More often than not this was obscure ... All this frequently led to local misunderstandings, and has not by any means even now removed discrepancies in the solution of the matter.'[165]

Attempts to put pressure on the *kolkhozniks* to liquidate their plots still occur. One of the main party journals recently held up as an example a *kolkhoz* which, 'on the decision of the *kolkhozniks*', bought all their cows and reduced the size of their plots.[166] The tug-of-war continues between peasants who, by various ruses, attempt illegally to expand their plots at the expense of the farms, and the authorities, who do their best to unmask such practices.[167] The plots are also the centre of a controversy over labour-discipline: 'Some *kolkhoz* chairmen consider the reduction of *kolkhoz* household private plots to be the basic method of strengthening labour discipline.'[168] But reformers are trying to get this form of sanction abolished when the Model Statutes are revised.[169]

The post-Khrushchev régime would obviously prefer to shelve rather than tackle the whole thorny issue of the plots. But the pressure for reform will not abate, and the economic importance of the plots is so great that the régime cannot really avoid intervening.

VILLAGE LIFE

(a) RURAL DEPOPULATION

Almost half the Soviet population (107·1 million, or 46 per cent) is still classified as rural. Almost half this rural population

(52 million, or 48·6 per cent) is made up of *kolkhozniks*; the rest are State farmers, the 'rural intelligentsia', and the village bureaucracy.[170] Before the Second World War, Stalin set the target of drafting one-and-a-half million young *kolkhozniks* annually into industry.[171] The forced migration declined after the war, but was replaced by a spontaneous drift, especially of young people, from the villages to the towns. This exceeded expectations, and caused an alarming decline in the agricultural labour force. The First Secretary of the Pskov *obkom* told the March, 1965, plenum, for example, that between 1957 and 1964 able-bodied *kolkhozniks* in his *oblast* had declined from 200,000 to 110,000. If the trend continued, 'in ten years time there will be no able-bodied population in the *kolkhozes*'.[172] Pavlov, the Komsomol leader, told the plenum that 'in many *kolkhozes*' the average age of the labourers was over 50.[173]

According to a recent issue of *Party Life*, which expressed concern at 'this very serious matter', 'there are many hidden causes which impel young people to leave their home villages'.[174]

A survey into the 'anxieties of the Smolensk region' revealed some of them.[175] The investigators singled out the following, in order of importance:

(1) ' "the higher the educational level, the more sharply the prestige of the village . . . falls"; those who go, or are forced to go, to towns for specialised education (even in agricultural subjects) are likely to remain there;

(2) 'there are no fixed hours in the countryside . . . manual labour predominates and pay is low. People write: "I see my mother working from early morning to late at night and I am not attracted by the prospect"; "the same work pays more in the town than in the village. It is difficult to live on low earnings";

(3) 'the low level of cultural and everyday services . . . In conversations with the young people, they complained about this even more than the other two causes.'

Other social pressures were important. Even if a teenager resisted the temptations of town life to begin with, on finishing his national service

'he will either be recruited for a construction job . . . or will marry a town girl, or be talked around by his comrades or "come to his senses" by himself, but he will never return to his native village. . . . And once the young men have gone, the girls will also leave—they do not want simply to wither on the vine. Through the force of objective circumstances, through distortion of the sexual structure, we have simply been "driving" girls out of the villages . . .

'No sooner has one member of the family left and settled in town than he turns into a magnet attracting the growing members of the family one by one. Only the old people remain behind, the parents serving as caretakers in the deserted dwellings which the others may visit to rest in the lap of nature.'

Life in towns for the new migrants is frequently difficult. Even though labour reserves exist in the countryside (in many areas there is a pool of under-employed or seasonal workers) they are frequently unable to find employment in towns, according to one writer, who refers to the calculations of economists which demonstrate the 'very limited' possibilities of absorption into industry 'in the coming 10–15 years'.[176]

Various remedies for the problem of rural depopulation have been proposed, but as Aleksandr Yanov, a frank writer on rural themes, has recently pointed out:

'Practice proves indisputably that when applied individually, outside the whole complex of social, political and cultural problems facing the countryside today, these measures basically "won't work". Educated village youngsters leave clubs, good housing and prosperity. Obviously they are not satisfied by enough to eat, a roof overhead and dances in the clubs.'[177]

An earlier article by Yanov and another writer quoted a Smolensk farm chairman on the long-term economic, but more particularly psychological, answer:

'The forces of the towns should be put at the service of the land. All their progressive engineering thought, all their means of propaganda and agitation should work to raise the prestige of the countryside. Only on such a basis can the rural young be brought to love the land.'[178]

(b) CONSUMER GOODS AND SERVICES

Until the post-Khrushchev régime abolished it at the end of 1965, there was a special price mark-up of about seven per cent for various consumer goods sold in rural areas, on the grounds that marketing and transport costs were higher.[179]

Inequities remain, however, in the shape of an 'obsolete

system of supplying goods' to the rural shops.[180] The chairman of the Russian Federation's Consumer Co-operatives provided figures which demonstrated that 'a significant section of the rural population (30–40 per cent) is forced to acquire many necessities in the towns'.[181] One of the most frequent complaints aired in the Soviet Press is the unavailability of consumer goods in country areas. One recent article has pointed to the advantages of cutting out one of the stages in the present system (the State wholesale depôt which forces the shops to take whatever it thinks fit) and of developing a system of direct contracts between consumers' co-operatives and factories. This is opposed by the Ministry of Trade because it would mean a reduction in the number of employees in the State trading system.[182]

The standard of the service industries is far lower in the countryside than in the towns. In 1964, services of an industrial character performed in urban areas per head of the population were 4.4 times more than those performed in rural areas, and services of a non-industrial character were 8·4 times more:

'The shortage of servicing enterprises, the poor organisation of their work in servicing the rural population, the high price of their work, lead to the fact that the rural population primarily makes use of the services of private people.'[183]

In 1967, it was stated that a rural inhabitant of the RSFSR has six times fewer services than urban dwellers. In Turkmenia the corresponding figure was 17 times fewer.[184]

(c) CULTURAL AMENITIES

According to a speaker at the March, 1965, plenum: 'Not only material conditions but the state of cultural and ordinary living conditions of people in the country is far behind that in the towns. This difference is not diminishing, but increasing. Living conditions in the village stay what they were many years ago.'[185] It is commonly agreed that the low standard of cultural amenities has a bearing on the exodus into the towns (although it has also been said that 'it would be difficult to find an instance in which a club has kept young people in the countryside'[186]). One of the main focal centres of 'cultural' activity is the village clubhouse—over 111,000 of which exist.[187] But many are inaccessible: a third of the rural inhabitants of the RSFSR cannot visit them, for example, because of the distances involved.[188] The premises frequently leave a great deal to be desired:

'In many cases these are former churches, *kulak* houses or warehouses in an extremely ancient, sometimes tumbledown state, poorly equipped, unheated and without elementary conditions for people's leisure.'[189]

Even where new ones exist,

'as a rule there is still no proper work in them and "no films are shown" through the year.'[190]

The main reason is the extreme shortage of 'cultural workers'.

Ninety per cent of those who answered a questionnaire in the Voronezh region declared that 'nothing' pleased them in their clubs.[191] When it came to preferences, film shows and dances topped the poll: an 'amazingly minute' number of people preferred the functions with overtones of political indoctrination, like 'Question and Answer Evenings'. Despite such evidence, ideological functionaries still issue pronouncements of this nature:

'Not infrequently socio-political work is poorly provided for in clubs. People do not know how to organise debates or to attract young people to an evening of discussion on a subject. But all this must take place in a club!'[192]

(d) HOUSING AND RURAL DEVELOPMENT

One of the most constant complaints concerns the lack of building materials. It is common for the funds allocated by the State to *kolkhozes* for the purchase of these materials not to be used up, and the lack of material gives rise to much illicit 'acquisition'.[193]

At the March, 1965, plenum the delegate from Tambov *oblast* remarked that 'an especially grievous situation with regard to housing is growing up in villages in treeless areas ... the *izbas* (traditional wooden dwellings) are falling apart, and we are not allowed to sell even a cubic metre of timber'. The Kirgiz party First Secretary said:

'Only 19 per cent of the population of the Republic's State farms at the moment have their own living accommodation from State funds. Over 7,000 teachers, doctors and other specialists working in small areas have no assured accommodation. . . . A large proportion of rural inhabited points, particularly in mountainous areas, are entirely without amenities, and in the villages cramped mud huts predominate. . . . The overwhelming majority of livestock-workers live in *yourts* (nomadic-type tents), tents or in accommodation which does not meet elementary requirements.'[194]

At the 23rd CPSU Congress in 1966, it was decided to set up Republican Ministries for Rural Construction. However, the situation does not appear to have changed much since then.[195]

The area covered by a farm is often immense, and the idea of concentrating dispersed settlements into larger villages with urban-type housing is periodically raised, though the prospects of achieving anything along these lines seem little better now than they were in the early 'fifties when Stalin squashed Khrushchev's '*agrogorod*' plan. A current plan aims to select 120,000 of the 600–700,000 existing rural settlements for development

'in order that the remaining 480 or 580,000 become non-existent. The inhabitants of neighbouring settlements will have to move into the settlements with a future where all the amenities of town life will be created.'[196]

Allusion is openly made to the 'ideological "basis"' underlying one aspect of the question—the separation of the peasant from his private plot by putting him in a multi-storeyed house, often together with other families:

'The higher he is raised above the ground, the further he is from private property.'[197]

Under the pretext of resettlement plans some local authorities are forbidding the repair of existing homes, although the new settlements are as yet unbuilt.[198]

In some parts of the Soviet Union, notably the Baltic States, Belorussia and the Ukraine, collectivised peasant families continue to inhabit isolated farmsteads (*khutory*) surviving from the pre-collectivisation period. It is admitted that these scattered families pose difficulties for party indoctrination and political control.[199] Their resettlement in *kolkhoz* village centres was supposed to have been carried out even before the Second World War, but hardly any progress has been made.[200] The First Secretary of the Krasnodar *krai* party Committee recently complained that because of the widely scattered nature of small local settlements they did not as a rule possess party or Komsomol organisations. His party Committee was supporting 'the initiative of the *kolkhozes*' in concentrating their populations into larger settlements.[201]

Village life as a whole is, of course, particularly resistant to party ideology:

'Religious survivals are particularly tenacious among village dwellers by virtue of the presence of substantial differences between town and villages. Research into the state of religious belief in Belorussia has shown, for example, that the level of religious belief of the town population is half that of the rural population.'[202]

Rural isolation is to a large extent a consequence of a poor road system. A journalist recently exclaimed:

'Roads! Roads between settlements, roads—streets with pavements within villages! I am convinced that without this it is impossible to speak seriously not only about overcoming the considerable differences between the country and the town but also about the most elementary culture of the village.'[203]

Nearly 80 per cent of the roads in the RSFSR (which suffers more than some other Republics in this respect) are earth tracks 'essentially unsuitable for cars'.[204] For this reason alone, urban dwellers are likely to be the main beneficiaries of the recent, more indulgent policy towards the private car.

(e) SOCIAL SERVICES;
PENSIONS, TRADE UNIONS

In the provision of social services, the State spent only half as much on the rural population, per head, as on the urban, in 1959.[205]

Until recently, old age and disablement pensions, sickness, maternity and other benefits, and subsidised holidays, were only provided for rank-and-file collective farmers from collective farm funds (apart from one or two special categories of workers such as the war disabled). Since most *kolkhozes* had little money to spare, such services were inadequate. In any case, not more than two per cent of total income could be set aside for the provision of such services.[206] In 1957, less than four per cent of elderly collective farmers received a pension of any kind; by 1959 the figure was 14 per cent, but the average pension was only some 8 roubles per month compared to the stipulated minimum State pension of 30 roubles.[207] Soviet literary fiction of the period reflects the social injustice: in

[121]

Abramov's celebrated story *Round and About*, the first person to receive a pension in the history of the *kolkhoz*—a pension in kind at that—was an old woman reduced to begging.[208]

In 1964, action was finally taken to remedy the situation. A pension fund financed partly by the State and partly by the collective farms themselves was established. However, the guiding principles were strict:

'There must not be a levelling approach in providing pensions for collective farmers . . . Those *kolkhozniks* must be provided for better who work well and make a big contribution to communal production'.[209]

The *kolkhoznik's* minimum old-age pension was fixed at 12 roubles per month and his retirement age at 65. This compared badly with the minimum of 30 roubles, under the State pension law of 1956, for urban workers, who could retire at 60. In 1967, the retirement age was lowered to that of urban workers: 60 for men and 55 for women, and certain other lesser improvements were made (such as an increase in minimum sickness benefits).[210]

Although the richer *kolkhozes* help to finance the less prosperous ones *via* the central fund, the old-age pensions are based on previous earnings for work on the farm over any five-year period in the ten years prior to retirement. Members of the many economically weak farms, in which the pay is low, thus continue to be badly off in their retirement as well.

Under a decree of July 20, 1964, *kolkhoz* chairmen, specialists, machine operators and technicians enjoy the more generous pension rights accorded industrial and State farm workers.[211] These are also the only categories which, since 1964, are entitled to join a trade union (to which all State farm workers have always belonged). Polyansky recognised recently that if ordinary *kolkhozniks* had the same social insurance and trade union rights as the State farmers and industrial workers, this would 'play a big rôle in erasing the social differences between the working class and the *kolkhoz* peasantry'. But he only held out a vague hope of achieving this when 'the time comes'.[212]

(f) EDUCATION

Educational facilities and opportunities have always been worse for rural children than those available to their urban contemporaries.

In 1967, 26 per cent of *kolkhozniks* were said to have had a secondary or higher education compared to 44 per cent of the working class.[213] A sociological analysis has pointed out that:

'the chance of young people who live in large towns entering a higher educational institute is much better than for those living in rural areas because the level of teaching in town schools is higher, as a rule'.[214]

The great disparity in educational opportunities available to children of the urban intelligentsia and of agricultural workers was shown in a survey of ten per cent of secondary school-leavers in the Novosibirsk *oblast* in 1963. Ninety-three per cent of the former and 76 per cent of the latter wished to proceed to further education; 82 per cent of the former did so, but only ten per cent of the latter. Two per cent of the former and ten per cent of the latter wished to proceed to work; 15 per cent of the former did so, but 90 per cent of the latter.[215]

In line with Khrushchev's policy of 'bringing education nearer to life', up to 80 per cent of places in higher educational establishments were reserved, after 1958, for applicants with two years' experience on production. In 1959, a decree, 'on the participation of industrial enterprises and State and collective farms in filling places in higher educational establishments and technical colleges to train specialists for their enterprises', entitled *kolkhozes* and *sovkhozes* to send farmworkers at the farms' expense to universities, etc., after which they returned to the farms.[216] The post-Khrushchev régime reversed this policy, which it found resulted in excessive discrimination against academically qualified applicants for higher education. It abolished the special quota of places for production workers, and although the farms apparently still have the right to select their own candidates, the latter must now pass entrance examinations.[217]

Even the statutory minimum period of primary schooling is not always completed and complaints that the shift system—up to three shifts daily—is still in force come predominantly from rural areas.[218]

At the 1967 session of the USSR Supreme Soviet, a delegate from a mountainous region revealed that teachers in small village schools were taking up to four classes simultaneously. Many schools had been shut, leaving children without educational facilities. Funds for building boarding schools were not forthcoming.[219] An article about conditions in the Omsk *oblast* revealed the low standards of teachers, particularly in rural areas, and the fact that 'a good half of the teachers do not stay in the villages'. Among the causes cited was the difference in town and rural customs—a smart young female teacher would be, for example, told to try and 'look like everyone else'.[220]

Material factors are, however, clearly pre-eminent among the reasons for understaffing. Despite an increase in salary in 1964, the teaching profession is still regarded as lowly paid. One teacher was quoted as saying in 1967 that any other profession was more profitable.[221] But the lack of housing—or suitable housing—is perhaps even more important. The main teachers' newspaper recently cited the case, for example, of a teacher living with her family of five in a nine-square-metre living space.[222] A local party Secretary suggested that there were some *kolkhoz* chairmen—extremely few, of course—who reasoned thus:

'What do I need ten-year teaching for? The children will learn, read their little books and run off to the town.'[223]

Similar attitudes may help to explain the reluctance of many farms to provide suitable amenities for teachers and pupils. Until September 1, 1965, the transport of schoolchildren in rural areas to and from school had to be paid for by their parents.[224] Pre-school facilities are also markedly poorer in the countryside.

Low educational standards are very much a feature of those who remain on the land. This is particularly true of the high proportion of unskilled labour to be found on *kolkhozes*. Some recent figures concerning a *kolkhoz* in the Ryazan region are instructive: of the workers in this lowest category, 4·3 per cent were illiterate, 79·5 per cent had only had a primary education, 14·6 per cent had an incomplete secondary education and a mere 1·6 per cent had completed their secondary education.[225]

One widespread practice often singled out for condemnation (in a 1966 party and government Resolution for example) is the employment of schoolchildren in fields during harvest time. The resolution forbids work 'not directly concerned with the educational process during school hours',[226] but in the past, rural authorities have claimed that such work is part of vocational training.

(g) HEALTH SERVICES

One of the perennial problems of the Soviet countryside is the disinclination of qualified people, like doctors and teachers, to live there. The authorities have the power to assign new graduates to any part of the Soviet Union, but young people frequently refuse to use their qualifications, preferring even menial work in towns. Those who do take the posts often leave them when their stint is over, even though there may be special financial inducements to stay in the areas in question. A Chekhovian sense of isolation pervades one recent analysis of a village in the Kostroma area:

'Ninety *intelligenty* [not necessarily "intellectuals": the concept merges with that of "white-collar workers"] live in Andreevsky. Surely they have opportunities for intellectual contacts, for consolidating into another ... social group in village society ... But the point is that such a group is lacking in the village. The teachers keep to themselves, the medical people to themselves, the [agricultural] specialists as well. They do not in any way feel themselves to be a united force, the representatives of modern science and thought, and still less do they feel themselves to be an influential group in the village community. Can one be surprised? They can spend the whole of their lives living and working in this community ... but nine out of ten of them are not *kolkhoz* members and have no decisive voice at its meetings.'[227]

In 1967, there were said to be only one-ninth as many doctors and one-third as many hospital beds for every 10,000 rural inhabitants as for the same number of town-dwellers.[228] Under the 1959–65 Seven-Year Plan, it was official policy to encourage *kolkhozes* to build cottage-hospitals and maternity homes out of their own resources. Many medical posts are thus only staffed by relatively unqualified medical auxiliaries called *feldshers* and by nurses and midwives. However, there is now pressure for more State aid in building larger, well-equipped hospitals. At the March, 1965, plenum it was stated that despite the increase in the number of medical establishments, they did not correspond to 'the minimum demands'.[229] In particular, the lack of specialised treatment is deplored.[230]

There have in the past been reports of refusals by town hospitals to treat rural patients and also of refusals by *kolkhoz* chairmen to provide transport in urgent cases.[231]

(h) ELECTRIFICATION

The physical immensity of the Soviet Union helps to explain the relatively slow spread of electrification to *kolkhozes*. Until as late as 1958, only 49 per cent received electricity *via* the grid or their own generating stations. However, the percentage has risen rapidly: in 1966, it was claimed that 95 per cent of collective farms were making use of electricity for production purposes.[232] The same source made it clear that only 76 per cent of the homes of collective and State farmers had electricity in 1966.

In a well-known documentary story published at the end of 1962, A. Yashin contrasted two villages:

'In the large village of Sushinovo there was still no electricity, no radio, no library, no club.'

However:

'The village of Gribaevo was already connected to relayed wireless; next to the ikon-shelf hung the body of a loudspeaker and electric light burned under the ceiling. The proximity of an industrial scheme was evident in everything. It is true that in order for the light to shine with sufficient strength one had to screw in bulbs of 150 candlepower and lower voltage.'[233]

At the March, 1965, plenum the Belorussian party First Secretary revealed that in his Republic a third of the *kolkhoz* households 'cannot use electricity even for lighting their homes'.[234] An *oblast* party Secretary spoke of the Pskov area thus:

'About 70 per cent of the rural population in the collective farms does not possess electric lighting and makes use of kerosene lamps, moreover often without lamp-glass. It is evident that certain workers in the planning organs are so divorced from life that they consider the electrification of villages to be completed and have stopped planning the production of lamp-glass in the necessary quantities. The population, especially young people, cannot reconcile itself to such living conditions in the villages. It leaves the villages and tries to go where material and living conditions are better.'[235]

(i) MECHANISATION

Soviet agriculture is still under-mechanised. This was emphasised by several speakers at the March, 1965, plenum. In the Volgograd *oblast*, where early sowing of grain crops is particularly important, farms are unable to achieve it, according to the party First Secretary, 'because of shortage of cultivators, grain-sowers and even harrows. Things got so bad, comrades, that in the last four to five years these most simple agricultural machines were no longer sold to the collective and State farms according to their requirements, but were rationed out.'[236]

In the Rostov *oblast*, in 1965, a minimum of 17,000 tractors were needed to carry out ploughing according to scientific requirements, but only 11,500 were available. There was a similar shortage of other machinery.[237]

Even when machinery is available, it is sometimes a doubtful asset. The head of *Soyuzselkhoztekhnika* told the plenum about a seed-drilling attachment for the K700 tractor, which required for its maintenance the daily greasing of 212 points —an operation taking five hours. Many tractors, he said, required daily greasing and maintenance occupying a quarter of each working day.[238] Difficulty in obtaining spare parts is another notorious problem. In 1966, the Ministry of Tractor and Agricultural Machine-building underfulfilled its planned production of spare parts by over 7 million items, and the Ministry of the Automobile Industry by 6 million items. *Soyuzselkhoztekhnika* carried out a sample check of the spare parts supplied to its warehouses, and found over half of those checked—1,344,000—defective.[239]

One of the arguments originally put forward by the party for large-scale farming, in State and collective farms, was that they would be able to make fullest use of modern agricultural machinery—especially tractors. And yet, more than 30 years after collectivisation, Soviet industry is still unable to provide the farms with the necessary machines and technical supplies:

'At the present time the industry of the USSR is still not in a position to satisfy the constantly growing demand of the countryside for the necessary machines, mechanical equipment, chemicals and other materials. This will apparently require some time yet.'[240]

For the farmworkers, the lack of machinery often means unremitting drudgery, much of it performed by women, and in harsh climatic conditions. In 1965, some 95 per cent of all *kolkhozniks* were engaged in predominantly physical labour.[241] In 1967, 80 per cent lacked any form of 'professional training' (e.g. as tractor drivers or combine operators), and were 'occupied primarily in manual labour'.[242] Hand-tools such as shovels and rakes are designed and produced only for use by men. One economist has found it necessary to warn against 'ignoring the interests of the almost 16 million army of female agricultural workers, on whose shoulders has lain the main burden of unskilled labour in the communal economy and on the private plots'.[243]

A journalist recently stated:

'Out of every hundred *kolkhoz* and *sovkhoz* cows, 73 are still milked by hand, and about half watered by hand because there are no water pipes. As for the distribution of fodder and gathering of manure, the main mechanical aids are still in general the shovel and fork.'[244]

Even a job belonging by definition to women—that of milkmaid—is very arduous. The journalist already quoted once established that a milkmaid in charge of 14 cows (an average figure) has to perform some 8,000 'difficult movements' in milking daily.

'And apart from that, the milkmaid has to feed and water and clean the cows and muck out and carry heavy churns and wash them out and sterilise them with steam. And to do this she has to get up at four or, if she lives a long way off, at three o'clock in the morning in order to arrive in time for the morning milking; she finally gets back at ten or even eleven o'clock. And if she has a family (and I have written more than once that precisely because of milkmaids' working conditions family life often does not work out), she has either to neglect her family or her work.'[245]

SOURCES

1. *Pravda*, March 6, 1954.
2. This situation leads to some equivocal formulae in Soviet textbooks, e.g., 'brigadiers are on the *nomenklatura* of the party *raikom*, therefore the removal of a brigadier from his post can take place with the agreement of the party *raikom*' (*Kolkhoznoe Pravo*, p. 459).
3. *Izvestiya*, August 16, 1967.
4. *Pravda*, February 25, 1960.
5. Decree of March 1, 1965 (*Spravochnik Partiinogo Rabotnika*, 1966, p. 161).
6. *Selskaya Zhizn*, June 24, 1965.
7. *Lunev*, p. 315.
8. *Ibid.*, p. 311.
9. *Ibid.*, p. 320.
10. Sorokin, p. 72. There has, however, been a long, and so far fruitless, discussion about the need to place the

raion agricultural administration under dual subordination (*Sovetskoe Gosudarstvo i Pravo*, 1965, No. 10, p. 15; 1967, No. 8, p. 102).

11. Lunev, p. 312.
12. *Ibid.*, p. 319.
13. *Ibid.*, p. 313.
14. Decree of March 1, 1965 (*Spravochnik Partiinogo Rabotnika*, 1966, p. 163).
15. Lunev, p. 247.
16. Sorokin, p. 283; RSFSR *Laws*, 1924, 28: 266.
17. ESP, p. 309.
18. *Neva*, 1963, No. 1, pp. 130–1.
19. *Pravda*, July 21, 1965.
20. *Literaturnaya Gazeta*, December 27, 1967.
21. *Kolkhoznoe Pravo*, p. 133.
22. *Ekonomicheskaya Gazeta*, August 4, 1965, p. 30; *Sotsialisticheskaya Zakonnost*, 1967, No. 12, p. 47.
23. *SSSR v tsifrakh v 1966 godu*, p. 109; *Moscow News*, Supplement, 1967, No. 40, p. 18.
24. *Izvestiya*, August 11, 1967.
25. *SSSR v tsifrakh v 1966 godu*, p. 109.
26. *Moscow News*, Supplement, 1967, No. 40, p. 18.
27. *Narkhoz*, 1965, pp. 277, 288.
28. *Ibid.*, p. 435.
29. Zaslavskaya, p. 105.
30. *Ibid.*, p. 140.
31. *Ibid.*, p. 105.
32. ESKh., 1967, No. 2, pp. 10–11.
33. *Spravochnik*, pp. 49–51.
34. *Ibid.*, pp. 105–7.
35. Plenum, p. 28.
36. ESP, p. 400.

37. *Ibid.*, p. 184.
38. *Ibid.*
39. *Vedomosti RSFSR*, 1965, No. 43.
40. *Sotsialisticheskaya Zakonnost*, 1967, No. 1.
41. *Bakinsky Rabochy*, December 9, 1967.
42. ESP, p. 30. Under Khrushchev, the brigadier was supposed to participate in the work (*Kolkhoznoe Pravo*, p. 336).
43. ESP, p. 143.
44. *Kolkhoznoe Pravo*, p. 351.
45. *Ibid.*, p. 352.
46. *Ibid.*, p. 371.
47. *Voprosi Ekonomiki*, 1966, No. 10, pp. 64–5.
48. *Spravochnik*, p. 93; *Kolkhoznoe Pravo*, p. 370.
49. *Voprosi Ekonomiki*, 1966, No. 10, p. 65.
50. *Kolkhoznoe Pravo*, p. 349. This Decree replaced an earlier one, of March 3, 1936 (IKP, Vol. 1, p. 478), which made the NKVD responsible for organising the *corvée*. It appears at that time to have been regarded simply as another form of police-controlled forced labour.
51. *Spravochnik*, pp. 101–2.
52. Model Statutes, Article 17 (*Spravochnik*, p. 49).
53. *Spravochnik*, p. 58.
54. Decree of December 29, 1961 (*Pravda*, December 30, 1961).
55. Zaslavskaya, p. 104.
56. Plenum, p. 164.
57. *Novy Mir*, 1964, No. 1, p. 91.
58. *Kolkhoznoe Pravo*, p. 352.
59. *Spravochnik*, p. 99.

60. *Kommunist*, 1967, No. 15, p. 20 (Polyansky).
61. *Ibid.*
62. *Sovetskaya Rossiya*, January 29, 1965.
63. *Izvestiya*, September 26, 1967.
64. *Sovetskaya Yustitsiya*, 1967, No. 22, p. 10.
65. Zaslavskaya, p. 131.
66. *Voprosy Ekonomiki*, 1965, No. 7, pp. 27–8.
67. *Ibid.*, p. 35.
68. Plenum, pp. 143–4. The comparison presumably does not take into account *kolkhozniks'* earnings from their private plots. In 1964, actual pay per working day in agriculture was slightly over half what it was in industry, and in the *kolkhozes* it was about half. The average annual income of a *kolkhoznik* from his *kolkhoz* was 53 per cent of a State farm worker's income from his State farm. If income from his private plot were taken into account, the *kolkhoznik* still got ten per cent less than the State farmer per working day, and almost one-and-a-half times less than the average industrial wage (Zaslavskaya, pp. 39–40, 62).
69. *Pravda*, March 30, 1966.
70. *Pravda*, May 18, 1966.
71. Golikov, p. 9.
72. *Politicheskoe Samoobrazovanie*, 1968, No. 2, p. 124.
73. Zaslavskaya, p. 135.
74. *Ibid.*, pp. 183–4.
75. *Ibid.*, p. 189.
76. ESKh, 1967, No. 12, p. 72.
77. ESKh, 1967, No. 3, p. 85.
78. *Kommunist*, 1967, No. 15, p. 29.
79. *Izvestiya*, October 10, 1967.
80. Pankratov, p. 289.
81. The latest available figure is 196 days a year in 1964, for an adult, able-bodied *kolkhoznik* (Zaslavskaya, p. 40). The figure may have fallen with the subsequent removal of restrictions imposed by Khrushchev on the private plots.
82. *Ekonomicheskaya Gazeta*, 1968, No. 9, p. 16.
83. Zaslavskaya, p. 43.
84. RSFSR *Laws*, 1917, 1:3 (IKP, Vol. I, p. 17).
85. RSFSR *Laws*, 1919, 4:43 (IKP, Vol. I, p. 25).
86. IKP, Vol. I, p. 32.
87. BSE, second edition, Vol. 39, p. 542.
88. Hubbard, p. 78.
89. KPSS, Vol. 2, p. 391.
90. BSE, second edition, Vol. 39, p. 542.
91. Stalin, Vol. 13, p. 323.
92. Jasny, p. 787.
93. Stalin, Vol. 13, p. 329.
94. Volin, p. 76.
95. *Narkhoz*, 1964, p. 408.
96. *Selskaya Zhizn*, September 16, 1967 (Volovchenko).
97. *Arkhitektura SSSR*, 1956, No. 1.
98. *Kommunist*, 1956, No. 18 (Benediktov).
99. BSE, second edition, Vol. 39, p. 543.
100. *Ibid.*
101. *The Road to Communism*, p. 524.
102. Plenum, p. 27.
103. Sorokin, p. 79.

104. Piskunov and Polyakova, p. 108.
105. *Pravda Ukrainy*, November 17, 1965.
106. Piskunov and Polyakova, pp. 107, 109, 113.
107. *Narkhoz*, 1965, pp. 424, 443.
108. *Pravda*, January 26, 1968.
109 Popov-Cherkasov, pp. 29, 210–11.
110. *Ibid.*, p. 12.
111. *Ibid.*, p. 11.
112. *Ibid.*
113. *Ibid.*, p. 34.
114. *Pankratov*, p. 318.
115. Dmitrashko, p. 138.
116. *Ibid.*, p. 137.
117. *Ibid.*, p. 138.
118. Popov-Cherkasov, pp. 32–33.
119. Plenum, pp. 56–7.
120. *Spravochnik Partiinogo Rabotnika*, 1967, pp. 122–3.
121. Dmitrashko, p. 139.
122. Pankratov, pp. 299–300.
123. *Ibid.*, p. 302.
124. *Ibid.*, pp. 306–7.
125. *Ibid.*
126. *Ibid.*
127. BSE, second edition, Vol. 39, 542.
128. *Pravda*, February 3, 1955.
129. Plenum, p. 28.
130. *Kommunist*, 1956, No. 18, p. 73 (Benediktov).
131. ESKh, 1967, No. 12, p. 2.
132. *Izvestiya*, November 25, 1964.
133. *Sovetskaya Rossiya*, April 24, 1965.
134. *Kommunist*, 1966, No. 15, p. 79.
135. *Ibid.*
136. *Pravda*, December 10, 1964.
137. *Pravda Ukrainy*, November 17, 1965.
138. *Pravda*, April 15, 1967; ESKh, 1967, No. 12, p. 9.
139. ESKh, 1967, No. 12, p. 9.
140. *Kommunist*, 1966, No. 15, p. 83.
141. *Ibid.*
142. Zaslavskaya, p. 125.
143. *Sovetskoe Gosudarstvo i Pravo*, 1966, No. 3, p. 62; Lunev, p. 319.
144. Decree of April 1, 1965 (*Spravochnik Partiinogo Rabotnika*, 1966, p. 173).
145. *Sovetskoe Gosudarstvo i Pravo*, 1966, No. 3, p. 63.
146. *Ibid.*
147. *Zaslavskaya*, p. 119.
148. Golikov, p. 263; ESKh, 1967, No. 4, p. 15.
149. Decree of January 4, 1966 (Pankratov, p. 113). In 1968 contracts were concluded by February 1 (*Selskaya Zhizn*, March 15, 1968).
150. *Selskaya Zhizn*, November 30, 1967. Before 1967 a single contract covered all deliveries.
151. *Ibid.*
152. Statutes on the procedure for concluding and executing contract agreements for agricultural produce, approved by the State Committee for Procurements on January 6, 1966 (Pankratov, p. 118).
153. Lunev, p. 318.
154. Golikov, p. 262.
155. *Bakinsky Rabochy*, December 9, 1967.
156. Golikov, pp. 261, 263.
157. *Sovetskoe Gosudarstvo i Pravo*, 1966, No. 3, p. 64.
158. *Partiinaya Zhizn*, 1968, No. 4, p. 12.

159. *Kommunist*, 1967, No. 15, p. 29.
160. ESKh 1967, No. 5, p. 68.
161. *Voprosi Ekonomiki*, 1966, No. 10, pp. 60–1; No. 11, p. 27; *Soviet Studies*, July, 1968, pp. 46, 137.
162. *Voprosi Ekonomiki*, 1966, No. 10, pp. 58–60; Zaslavskaya, p. 165.
163. *Voprosi Ekonomiki*, 1967, No. 5, p. 51.
164. *Voprosi Ekonomiki*, 1966, No. 10, p. 63.
165. *Sovetskaya Yustitsiya*, 1966, No. 6, p. 23.
166. *Partiinaya Zhizn*, 1968, No. 3, p. 47.
167. *Selskaya Zhizn*, November 4, 1965, published an RSFSR Decree condemning peasants who 'seize communal land in excess of the limits established for their private plots, or keep cattle in quantities above the established norms'; *Zarya Vostoka*, November 21, 1967, condemned others, who pretended to have been divorced in order to extend their private holdings.
168. *Sovetskaya Yustitsiya*, 1966, No. 2, p. 22.
169. *Ibid.*; *Sovetskoe Gosudarstvo i Pravo*, 1966, No. 7, pp. 102–3; *Sovetskaya Yustitsiya*, 1966, No. 6, pp. 22–4.
170. *Izvestiya*, August 11, 1967.
171. *XVIII S'ezd VKP (b)*, p. 119.
172. Plenum, p. 142.
173. *Ibid.*, p. 162.

174. *Partiinaya Zhizn*, 1968, No. 3, p. 49.
175. *Literaturnaya Gazeta*, July 23, 1966.
176. *Novy Mir*, 1966, No. 8, p. 161.
177. *Literaturnaya Gazeta*, December 7, 1967.
178. *Literaturnaya Gazeta*, July 26, 1966.
179. ESKh, 1967, No. 3, p. 21.
180. *Izvestiya*, August 25, 1967.
181. *Ibid.*
182. *Izvestiya*, January 9, 1968.
183. Plenum, pp. 167–8.
184. ESKh, 1967, No. 1, p. 39.
185. Plenum, p. 144.
186. *Literaturnaya Gazeta*, July 26, 1966.
187. ESKh, 1967, No. 3, p. 23.
188. Plenum, p. 166.
189. *Ibid.*
190. *Literaturnaya Gazeta*, November 1, 1967.
191. *Sovetskaya Kultura*, January 6, 1966.
192. *Sovetskaya Kultura*, December 28, 1967.
193. *Oktyabr*, 1967, No. 6, p. 161.
194. Plenum, pp. 56, 159.
195. *Literaturnaya Gazeta*, December 5, 1967 (Semenov), and February 21, 1968.
196. *Literaturnaya Gazeta*, August 30, 1967 (Chetunova).
197. *Literaturnaya Gazeta*, February 7, 1968.
198. *Literaturnaya Gazeta*, January 24, 1968.
199. Plenum, p. 138; Kovalev, pp. 108, 135–6, 140.
200. Decree of May 27, 1939 (IKP, Vol. 2, p. 107).

201. *Partiinaya Zhizn*, 1967, No. 15, p. 15.
202. *Vestnik Moskovskogo Universiteta*, Philosophy Series, 1967, No. 4, p. 30.
203. *Literaturnaya Gazeta*, August 30, 1967 (Chetunova).
204. *Izvestiya*, October 26, 1966.
205. *Puti Sozdaniya Izobiliya*, p. 63.
206. USSR *Laws*, 1935, 11:82, article 11c.
207. *Puti Sozdaniya Izobiliya*, pp. 67–9.
208. *Neva*, 1963, No. 1, p. 114.
209. *Pravda*, July 16, 1964.
210. Decree of September 26, 1967 (*Pravda*, September 27, 1967).
211. *Spravochnik Partiinogo Rabotnika*, 1966, p. 262.
212. *Kommunist*, 1967, No. 15, p. 20.
213. *Izvestiya*, August 11, 1967.
214. *Voprosy Filosofii*, 1965, No. 5, pp. 65–6.
215. *Ibid.*
216. *Pravda*, September 20, 1959.
217. *Pravda* and *Sovetskaya Rossiya*, March 20, 1965.
218. *Pravda*, October 27, 1967; *Uchitelskaya Gazeta*, April 18 and April 27, 1968.
219. *Zarya Vostoka*, October 14, 1967.
220. *Uchitelskaya Gazeta*, May 25, 1967.
221. *Sovetskaya Rossiya*, July 5, 1967.
222. *Uchitelskaya Gazeta*, January 23, 1968.
223. *Oktyabr*, 1967, No. 6, p. 147.
224. *Spravochnik Partiinogo Rabotnika*, 1966, p. 330.
225. *Vestnik Moskovskogo Universiteta*, Philosophy Series, 1967, No. 4, p. 17.
226. *Pravda*, November 19, 1966.
227. *Literaturnaya Gazeta*, December 27, 1967.
228. ESKh, 1967, No. 3, p. 27.
229. Plenum, p. 112.
230. *Sovetskaya Rossiya*, September 20, 1967.
231. *Selskaya Zhizn*, July 13, 1963; May 14, 1964.
232. *Selskaya Zhizn*, April 22, 1966 (Neporozhny).
233. *Novy Mir*, 1962, No. 12, pp. 11, 24.
234. Plenum, p. 75.
235. *Ibid.*, p. 144.
236. *Ibid.*, pp. 67–8.
237. *Ibid.*, p. 117.
238. *Ibid.*, p. 152.
239. *Pravda*, February 23, 1967.
240. ESKh, 1967, No. 2, p. 30.
241. *Voprosy Filosofii*, 1967, No. 12, p. 8.
242. *Izvestiya*, August 11, 1967.
243. *Voprosi Ekonomiki*, 1966, No. 10, p. 65.
244. *Zhurnalist*, 1967, No. 6, p. 19.
245. *Ibid.*

BIBLIOGRAPHY

Arkhitektura SSSR (Architecture of the USSR) periodical, organ of the USSR Union of Architects.

Bakinsky Rabochy (Baku Worker), newspaper of the Azerbaidjan Party Central Committee, Supreme Soviet and Council of Ministers.

Bolshaya Sovetskaya Entsiklopediya (Large Soviet Encyclopaedia), first edition, 65 vols. with supplementary volume on the USSR, Moscow, 1926–47; second edition, 51 vols. with supplementary volume on the USSR, Moscow, 1949–58. (Cited as BSE)

Conquest, R., *Power and Policy in the USSR*, Macmillan, London,

Danilov, V. P. (editor), *Ocherki Istorii Kollektivizatsii Selskogo Khozyaistva v Soyuznykh Respublikakh* (Outline History of the Collectivisation of Agriculture in the Union Republics), State Publishing House of Political Literature, Moscow, 1963.

Dethronement of Stalin, The, pamphlet published by the *Manchester Guardian*, June, 1956.

Dmitrashko, I. (editor), *Oplata Truda v Selskom Khozyaistve SSSR* (The Payment of Labour in Agriculture in the USSR), Publishing House of Social-Economic Literature, Moscow, 1962.

Dvoskin, B., and Sidorov, I., *Tselinny Krai* (The Virgin Lands), *Mysl* Publishing House, Moscow, 1964.

Ekonomicheskaya Gazeta (Economic Gazette), newspaper, organ of the Central Committee of the CPSU.

Ekonomika Selskogo Khozyaistva (The Economics of Agriculture), periodical of the Ministry of Agriculture. (Cited as ESKh)

Entsiklopedichesky Slovar Pravovykh Znanii (Encyclopaedic Dictionary of Legal Knowledge), 'Soviet Encyclopaedia' Publishing House, Moscow, 1965. (Cited as ESP)

Fainsod, M., *Smolensk Under Soviet Rule*, Macmillan, London, 1959.

Golikov, V. (editor), *Itogi i Perspektivy* (Results and Prospects), State Publishing House of Political Literature, Moscow, 1967.

Golyakov, I. T., *Ugolovnoe Pravo* (Criminal Law), Juridical Publishing House, Moscow, 1947.

Gsovski, V., *Soviet Civil Law*, two vols., University of Michigan Law School, 1948.

Hubbard, L., *The Economics of Soviet Agriculture*, Macmillan, London, 1939.

Istoriya Kolkhoznogo Pravo (A History of Kolkhoz Law), two vols., State Publishing House of Juridical Literature, Moscow, 1958. (Cited as IKP)

Istoriya Kommunisticheskoi Partii Sovetskogo Soyuza (History of the CPSU), State Publishing House of Political Literature, second edition, Moscow, 1962.

Izvestiya (News), newspaper, organ of the Presidium of the USSR Supreme Soviet.

Jasny, N., *The Socialised Agriculture of the USSR*, Stanford, California, 1949.

Karcz, J., and Timoshenko, V., *Soviet Agricultural Policy, 1953–1962*, Stanford, California, 1964.

Kolkhoznoe Pravo (Kolkhoz Law), textbook published by Moscow University, 1962.

Kollektivizatsiya Selskogo Khozyaistva (The Collectivisation of Agriculture), Publishing House of the USSR Academy of Sciences, Moscow, 1957. (Cited as KSKh)

Kommunist (Communist), periodical published by the Central Committee of the CPSU.

Kommunist (Communist), newspaper of the Armenian Party Central Committee, Supreme Soviet and Council of Ministers.

Komsomolskaya Pravda (Young Communist Truth), newspaper, organ of the Komsomol Central Committee.

Korovyakovsky, D. Z., *Sovershenstvovanie Sistemy Gosudarstvennykh Zagotovok Selskokhozyaistvennykh Produktov v SSSR* (Improving the System of State Deliveries of Agricultural Products in the USSR), Economic Literature Publishing House, Moscow, 1963.

Kovalev, S., *Selskoe Rasselenie* (Rural Settlement), Moscow University, Moscow, 1963.

KPSS v Rezolyutsiakh i Resheniyakh (The CPSU in Resolutions and Decisions), State Publishing House of Political Literature, two vols., seventh edition, Moscow, 1953–4. Cited as KPSS)

Lenin, V. I., *Sochineniya* (Works), fourth edition, 35 vols., Marx-Engels-Lenin Institute, Moscow, 1941–50.

Literaturnaya Gazeta (Literary Gazette), newspaper, organ of the Board of the USSR Union of Writers.

Lunev, A. (editor), *Administrativnoe Pravo* (Administrative Law), Juridical Literature Publishing House, Moscow, 1967.

Marx, Karl, and Engels, Friedrich, *Selected Works* in two vols., Lawrence and Wishart, London, 1950. (Cited as Marx and Engels)

[135]

Moscow News, newspaper, organ of the Union of Soviet Societies of Friendship and Cultural Relations with Foreign Countries.

Narodnoe Khozyaistvo SSSR v 1964 g. (Economy of the USSR in (1964), Statistical Handbook, Moscow, 1965. (Cited as *Narkhoz*, 1964)

Narodnoe Khozyaistvo SSSR v 1965 g. (Economy of the USSR in 1965), Statistical Handbook, Moscow, 1966. (Cited as *Narkhoz*, 1965)

Neva (The Neva), periodical, organ of the RSFSR Union of Writers and its Leningrad branch.

New Directions in the Soviet Economy (Studies prepared for a sub-committee of the US Congress), Part II B, Washington, 1966. (Cited as *New Directions*.)

Novy Mir (New World), periodical, organ of the USSR Union of Writers.

Oktyabr (October), periodical, organ of the RSFSR Union of Writers.

Pankratov, A. (editor), *Zakonodatelstvo o Proizvodstve, Zagotovkakh i Zakupkakh Selkhozproduktov* (Legislation on the Production, Deliveries and Procurements of Agricultural Products), Juridical Literature Publishing House, Moscow, 1967.

Partiinaya Zhizn (Party Life), periodical published by the Central Committee of the CPSU.

Piskunov, V., and Polyakova, N., *Ekonomika Selskokhozyaistvennykh Predpriyatii* (Economics of Agricultural Enterprises), Publishing House of Political Literature, Moscow, 1962.

Planovoe Khozyaistvo (Planned Economy), periodical published by USSR *Gosplan*.

Plenum Tsentralnogo Komiteta Kommunisticheskoi Partii Sovetskogo Soyuza 24–26 Marta 1965 g. (Plenum of the Central Committee of the CPSU, March 24–26, 1965), Publishing House for Political Literature, Moscow, 1965. (Cited as Plenum.)

Politicheskoe Samoobrazovanie (Political Self-Education), periodical, organ of the Central Committee of the CPSU.

Popov, N., *Outline History of the CPSU*, two vols., Co-operative Publishing Society of Foreign Workers in the USSR, Moscow-Leningrad, 1934.

Popov-Cherkasov, I., *et al.*, *Organizatsiya Zarabatnoi Platy Rabochikh v Sovkhozakh SSSR* (The Organisation of Wage Payments for State Farm Workers in the USSR), *Ekonomika* Publishing House, Moscow, 1964.

Pravda (Truth), newspaper, organ of the Central Committee of the CPSU.

Pravda Ukrainy (Truth of the Ukraine), newspaper, organ of the Ukrainian Party Central Committee, Supreme Soviet and Council of Ministers.

Prokopovicz, S.N., *Histoire Economique de l'URSS*, Flammarion, Paris, 1952.

Puti Sozdaniya Izobiliya Selskokhozyaistvennykh Produktov v SSSR (Ways of Creating an Abundance of Agricultural Produce in the USSR), handbook, Economic Literature Publishing House, Moscow, 1963.

Road to Communism, The (Documents of the 22nd Party Congress), Foreign Languages Publishing House, Moscow, no date (1962?).

RSFSR Laws:
1917–38: *Sobranie Uzakoneniy i Rasporyazheniy Raboche-Krestyanskogo Pravitelstva Rossiyskoy Sovetskoy Federativnoy Sotsialisticheskoy Respubliki* (Collection of Statutes and Orders of the Worker-Peasant Government of the Russian Soviet Federative Socialist Republic), People's Commissariat of Justice of the RSFSR, Moscow.

Selskaya Zhizn (Village Life), newspaper, organ of the Central Committee of the CPSU.

Selskoe Khozyaistvo (Agriculture), former newspaper, organ of the Ministry of Agriculture.

Sharova, P. N., *Kollektivizatsiya Selskogo Khozyaistva v Tse Che O* (The Collectivisation of Agriculture in the Central Black Earth *Oblast*), Publishing House of the USSR Academy of Sciences, Moscow, 1963.

Sorokin, V. (editor), *Sovetskoe Administrativnoe Pravo* (Soviet Administrative Law), Leningrad University, Leningrad, 1966.

Sotsialisticheskaya Zakonnost (Socialist Legality), periodical, organ of the Prosecutor's Office of the USSR.

Sotsialisticheskoe Zemledelie (Socialist Agriculture), former newspaper, organ of the Ministry of Agriculture.

Sotsialistichesky Vestnik, Menshevik *émigré* periodical, Berlin, Paris, New York, 1921–65.

Sovetskaya Istoricheskaya Entsiklopediya (The Soviet Historical Encyclopaedia), ten vols. published so far by 'Soviet Encyclopaedia' Publishing House, Moscow, 1961–. (Cited as SIE.)

Sovetskaya Kultura (Soviet Culture), newspaper, organ of the Ministry of Culture and the Central Committee of the Trade Union of Cultural Workers.

Sovetskaya Rossiya (Soviet Russia), newspaper, organ of the Central Committee of the CPSU.

Sovetskaya Yustitsiya (Soviet Justice), periodical, organ of the Ministry of Justice and the Supreme Court of the RSFSR.

Sovestskoe Gosudarstvo i Pravo (Soviet State and Law), periodical published by the Institute of State and Law of the USSR Academy of Sciences.

Soviet Studies, quarterly, edited at the University of Glasgow, and published by Basil Blackwell, Oxford.

Spravochnik Partiinogo Rabotnika (Party Worker's Handbook), Publishing House of Political Literature, Moscow, 1966, 1967.
Spravochnik po zakonodatelsvu dlya Kolkhoznika (Handbook on Legislation for the *Kolkhoznik*), State Publishing House of Juridical Literature, Moscow, 1961. (Cited as *Spravochnik*.)
SSSR v Tsifrakh v 1966 Godu (The USSR in Figures in 1966), statistical handbook, Moscow, 1967.
Stalin, J. V., *Sochineniya* (Works), 13 vols., Marx-Engels-Lenin Institute, Moscow, 1946–51; Vols. 14–16, Hoover Institution, Stanford, California, 1967.

Uchitelskaya Gazeta (Teachers Gazette), newspaper, organ of the Ministry of Education and of the Central Committee of the Trade Union of Workers in Education, Higher Schools and Scientific Establishments.
USSR Laws:
    1924–38: *Sobranie Zakonov i Rasporyazheniy Raboche-Krestyanskogo Pravitelstva Soyuza Sovetskikh Sotsialisticheskikh Respublik* (Collection of Laws and Orders of the Worker-Peasant Government of the Union of Soviet Socialist Republics), Administration of Affairs of the Council of People's Commissars of the USSR, Moscow.

Vedomosti Verkhovnogo Soveta RSFSR (Gazette of the RSFSR Supreme Soviet), organ of the Supreme Soviet of the RSFSR. (Cited as Vedomosti RSFSR.)
Vestnik Moskovskogo Universiteta (Herald of Moscow University), periodical published by Moscow University.
Vestnik Statistiki (Statistical Herald), periodical, organ of the Central Statistical Administration.
Volin, L., *A Survey of Soviet Russian Agriculture*, US Department of Agriculture, 1951.
Voprosi Ekonomiki (Questions of Economics), periodical, organ of the USSR Academy of Sciences.
Voprosi Filosofii (Questions of Philosophy), periodical, organ of the USSR Academy of Sciences.
Voprosi Istorii (Questions of History), periodical, organ of the USSR Academy of Sciences and the Ministry for Higher and Special Secondary Education.
Voznesensky, N., *Voennaya Ekonomika SSSR* (The War Economy of the USSR), State Publishing House of Political Literature, Moscow, 1948.
Vyshinsky, A. Ya., *Revolyutsionnaya Zakonnost na Sovremennom Etape* (Revolutionary Legality at the Present Stage), Moscow, 1933.

XVIII S'ezd VKP(b), Stenograficheski Otchet (18th Congress of the All-Union Communist Party (Bolsheviks), stenographic report), State Publishing House of Political Literature, Moscow, 1939.

XXIII S'ezd KPSS, Stenograficheski Otchet (23rd Congress of the SPSU, stenographic report), two vols., State Publishing House of Political Literature, Moscow, 1966.

Zarya Vostoka (Dawn of the East), newspaper, organ of the Georgian Party Central Committee, Supreme Soviet and Council of Ministers.

Zaslavskaya, T., *Raspredelenie po Trudu v Kolkhozakh* (Distribution According to Work in the Kolkhozes), *Ekonomika* Publishing House, Moscow, 1966.

Zhurnalist (The Journalist), periodical published by *Pravda* and the Union of Journalists.